Position of Jilin in China

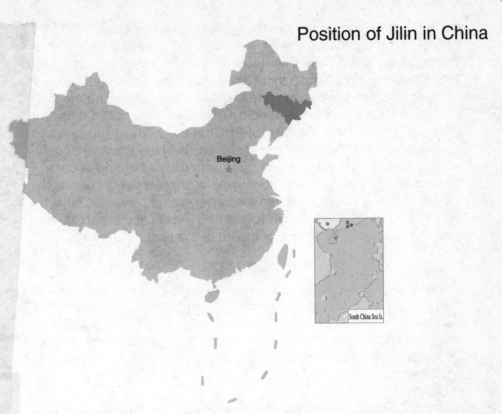

Beijing

South China Sea Is.

Sketch Map of Jilin

Baicheng

Songyuan

Changchun

Jilin

Korean Autonomous Prefecture
of Yanbian

Siping

Liaoyuan

Baishan

The sacred Changbai Mountain.

Tianchi (Heavenly Pool) in spring.

Walking in a world of snow. ▷

CONTENTS

Songhua River — Jilin's Mother River

Foreword

Located at the center of Northeast Asia, Jilin Province of northeast China covers an area of about 190,000 square kilometers. Jilin Province boasts two famed landscapes — Changbai Mountain and Songhua River, composing a magnificent natural scenic panorama. The river has shaped the mountain, while the mountain is the source of the river.

Beautiful Changbai Mountain lies to the east of Jilin Province, featuring a profound historical and cultural background. It has given birth to three meandering rivers, namely, Songhua River, Tumen River and Yalu River, which wind on and on, like colored ribbons on the land of Jilin. Various kinds of plants and medicinal herbs grow on this magnificent mountain. Also the home to many birds and beasts, the mountain offers protection to the northeast China plains, the largest granary of China.

Originating from Tianchi (Heavenly Pool), the Songhua River gathers to itself more than

920 tributeries along the way, eventually joining the Heilongjiang River and flowing into the Sea of Okhotsk. This richly endowed river flows over 1,000 km down through Jilin Province, providing water for the crop fields, irrigating 10,000 hectares of fertile farmland. On both sides of it, forests, mineral resources, wetlands, soybeans and sorghum are to be seen everywhere.

As the father mountain and mother river that have nurtured generations of Jinlin people, Changbai Mountain and the Songhua River have become synonymous with Jinlin Province. Each place nurtures its own inhabitants, while the inhabitants nurture their own culture. Changbai Mountain and Songhua River's black soil has fostered the Jilin people, who have created a splendid multicultural milieu that has created a unique cultural vision to match the natural landscape.

Farmland on the central Jilin Plain.

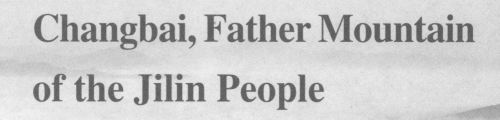

Changbai, Father Mountain of the Jilin People

Changbai:
the No. 1 Mountain in Northeast China

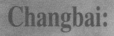

Changbai Mountain lies in east part of Liaoning, Jilin and Heilongjiang provinces, stretching across over 1,000 km. These days, Changbai Mountain and the Songhua River have become synonymous with northeast China.

A Sacred Mountain

Changbai Mountain has all along been held as a sacred place.

With a history of over 12,000,000 years, Changbai Mountains took shape before the famous orogenesis of the Himalayas Mountains. The earliest accounts of the mountain are found in the *Book of Mountains and Seas*, the oldest geographical record of China, dating back to over 4,000 years ago. Changbai Mountain is styled *"Buxian Shan"* in this classic. *"Buxian"* means "celestial being" in Mongolian language, so *"Buxian Shan"* implies "mountain with celestials."

Lofty Changbai Mountain was called "Greater Gaima Mountain" in the Han-Wei period, "Tutai Mountain" in the Northern and Southern Dynasties, and then "Taibai Mountain" in the Tang Dynasty. From the time of the Liao and Jin dynasties, the name "Changbai" (Ever White) became increasingly popular, which became the official in 1908, the 34th year of the reign period of Emperor Guangxu of Qing Dynasty.

Another history book records: the Wuji people living in northeast China more than 2,000 years ago held Changbai Mountain in great awe, calling it "Taihuang Mountain." At that time, people were not allowed to relieve themselves on the mountain unless they took the excrement away.

Northeast China used to be inhabited by many small tribes and ethnic groups successively, and they include the Sushen, Woju, Fuyu, Xianbei, Koguryo, Mongol and Qidan. In all their legends, Changbai Mountain was honored as a sacred mountain.

The Nüzhens (an ancient tribe in northeast China, later known as the Manchus), who founded the Jin Dynasty, regarded Changbai Mountain as their birthplace. They often paid homage to the mountain, devoutly hoping that fate would smile on their kingdom. In 1172, the ruler of the Jin Dynasty conferred an honorific title upon the mountain, and later a second title was given.

During the Qing Dynasty (1644-1911), the Manchu people's worship of Changbai Mountain reached its height. Legend has it that the forebears of the Aisin Gioro clan, imperial clan of the Qing, was born from the female immortal of Changbai Mountain who had swallowed a magical fruit. Thus, Changbai Mountain has been treasured as a sacred land, symbolizing the prosperity of the Qing Dynasty. Wicker fences were set up to enclose hillsides for livestock grazing, hunting, and ginseng digging. Thereafter, Emperor Kangxi sent envoys to visit the mountain. In 1677, the emperor arrived at the banks of the Songhua River on an inspection tour of the east, gazed upon the mountain, and conferred a title on it, announcing that Changbai Mountain should be worshiped every year as solemnly as the Five Sacred Mountains. Since then, successive Qing emperors all adhered to the system passed down by their ancestors, worshiped Changbai Mountain in different ways and composed numerous poems about it. Emperor Yongzheng even built a palace on Xiaobai Mountain in Jilin for this purpose.

People living in northeast China today are still filled with the same appreciation of it. Changbai Mountain is the source of the three main rivers in the northeast: Songhua, Tumen and Yalu rivers. Providing a protective natural barrier for this region, it is a cradle of agriculture and industry, where people have lived and multiplied for generations.

The great mountain adorned in white.

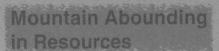

Changbai, Father Mountain
of the Jilin People

Mountain Abounding in Resources

Changbai Mountain is a dormant volcano. It erupted several times in history, giving rise to unique land formations. Changbai Mountain is beautiful, towering and primeval. It has been cherished as a sacred mountain whose hillsides were closed off during the Qing Dynasty. As a result, the natural resources and landscape remained in fairly good condition. Up to now, Changbai Mountain has maintained its primeval features, such as the vast expense of virgin forests, a gigantic high-altitude lake, a majestic waterfall, groups of hot springs, and green high-altitude tundra.

Changbai Mountain is not only characterized by its enchanting beauty, but also by its rich resources and biodiversity. With Tianchi (Heavenly Pool) at its center, the Changbai Mountain Nature Reserve, covering a total

Volcanic terrain in Changbai Mountain.

11

of 190,000 hectares, is one of China's mammoth natural reserves. It features the best-preserved virgin forests. Changbai, a treasure mountain, is one of China's three treasure-houses of natural resources, as well as an important gene bank of species. More than 1,000 kinds of plants and medicinal herbs grow in this area. It is also home to many birds and beasts, holding the most abundant sources of wild animals and plants in northern Eurasia. Today, Changbai Mountain is playing a more and more important role in the economic development of northeast China. Moreover, its dense forest vegetation helps regulate climate and rainfall, protecting the largest granary of China — the Northeast China Plains. According to ecologists, if there were no vast forests on Changbai Mountain, the Northeast China Plains would turn into barren land.

The renowned beautiful landscape, vast sea of forests and unique animal life have resulted in its inclusion in the UN International Biodiversity Protection Zone early in 1980. Changbai Mountain is

◄ The rhyme of snow in forest.

▲ A fox.

► Wild Manchurian tiger on Changbai Mountain.

one of the best-preserved nature reserves, acclaimed as a "natural museum" and "species bank." Once, a world famous ecologist visited Changbai Mountain, and he could hardly contain himself, claiming, "Changbai Mountain is one of the best-preserved nature reserves with intact primitive ecosystem. It is not only a wealth belonging to the Chinese people, but also for mankind."

▷ The primeval ecosystem of Changbai Mountain has been kept intact.

◁ Sika deer.

◁ A sable.

15

Tianchi (Heavenly Pool)

Tianchi (Heavenly Pool) is the highest volcanic lake in China, and is listed in the *Guinness Book of Records*. The lake is known for its sublime and mysterious natural beauty.

Tianchi lies in the southeast of Jilin Province, delineating the boundary between China and the Democratic People's Republic of Korea. Its northern part lies in Jilin Province. As the deepest natural lake in China, it is 373 meters at its maximum depth, averaging 204 m deep, and has an elevation of 2,189.1 m. Visitors transfer to cross-country vehicles halfway up the mountain to reach it. Those who are in good physical shape can travel on foot down the Tianchi Corridor, taking an hour and a half to arrive at the lake.

Water Flows Out Though No Water Flows In

Tianchi was originally called "Tumen Pool," meaning the origin of all rivers and lakes. The main rivers of the Northeast China Plains — Songhua, Tumen and Yalu — all originate from Changbai Mountain.

Hemmed in by 16 peaks, all of which are more than 2,500 m above sea level, Tianchi resembles a jasper gem mounted upon a chain of peaks. On bright sunny days, white clouds in the sky are mirrored on this giant bowl of sapphire water, and the beauty of the lake and sky becomes an integral whole. The climate on Changbai Mountain varies. Sometimes blurred in veils of mist, Changbai Mountain is faintly discernible. Although it is a pity that one cannot catch a full view of the lake, the misty scene is especially enchanting.

The surface of Tianchi appears as smooth as a mirror. Legend has it that the Queen Mother of the West, a popular goddess in Chinese mythology, had two lovely daughters. No one could decide who was more beautiful. The Great White Venus presented a treasured mirror to the Queen Mother at the Peach Banquet. The mirror said that the younger sister was more beautiful, which enraged the elder sister. She threw it from Jasper Lake. The mirror fell to Earth and turned into Tianchi.

Historical documents claimed that Tianchi had no ice in winter and no duckweed in summer. But actually, the lake freezes in winter. The average thickness of the ice sheet is 1.2 m, with the frozen season lasting six or seven months long. Fortunately, there are many hot springs in the lake, forming several hot-spring zones, 150 m long and 30-40 m wide. The temperature remains 42°C all year around. Even in mid-winter, visitors will be greeted by warm currents of air. Thus, Tianchi is also known as "Warm and Cold Pool."

Unlike other lakes, water keeps flowing out Tianchi; yet no water flows in. Large in size, the lake has a huge water storage, unparalleled among alpine lakes. However, it only has one water outlet, which is a U-shape breach between Longmen Peak and Tianhuo Peak at the northern end of the lake. The beach is over 20 m wide, where water rushes down, forming a 68-m-high waterfall. The uniqueness of the waterfall is that it keeps pouring out with the same volume of water all the year round, regardless of extreme heat or biting cold, dry season or rainy season.

How can this phenomenon be explained? Ancient people believed that the lake arose from the sea, giving it the name "Eye of the Sea." According to *Brief Records of Rivers and Ridges of Changbai Mountain*, "The lake is located at the center of the top of Changbai Mountain, surrounded by a chain of peaks, about 20 *li* high, so it is named 'Heavenly Pool.' Ancients said that the water did not rise and fall on ordinary days and the tide flows and ebbs every seven days. Connected to the sea, it is known as the 'Eye of the Sea'." In fact, there exists an altitudinal difference of over 2,000 m between Tianchi and the sea. So, how did the seawater come up? In addition, seawater is salty, whereas the water in the lake is totally different, feeling sweet and chilly.

According to *Dictionary of Place Names of Fusong County*, there are many beautiful legends in the long-standing history of Tianchi about the Dragon King and his

The beautiful Tianchi (Heavenly Pool).

palace. The surging lake produced a sound similar to copper gongs, often accompanied by a thunderclap, covering more than 100 *li*. Legend has it that this was caused by a great din of drums and pipes, and a drill conducted in the dragon king's palace. Besides, listening to music and training his soldiers, the dragon king of the lake also maintained close contact with the external world. One day in March, he entertained the dragon king of the Heilongjiang River, who mounted a black cloud and flew in from the northwest, bringing hail and rain to the lake. After spending a few days together, they mounted a white cloud and a black cloud respectively, circling Tianchi and then flew southeastward to make a pilgrimage to the dragon king of the East China Sea. About ten days later, the dragon king of Tianchi came back alone from the East China Sea, while the dragon king of the Heilongjiang River remained there to look after certain affairs. This is the famous story of the two dragon kings paying homage to the dragon king of East China Sea. Inhabited by the dragon king, Tianchi is also known as "Dragon Pond."

Groundwater, rainfall and melting make up the headwaters of Tianchi. Its soubriquet of "Eye of the Sea," along with the legends of the dragon king and his palace, only add to the mystery of the lake.

Tianchi (Heavenly Pool) in spring.

23

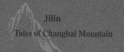
Monster in Tianchi

The Tianchi Monster, the Loch Ness Monster, the UFOs and the Bermuda Triangle which is associated with mysterious maritime accidents, are some of the world's greatest mysteries. Tales of the Tianchi Monster spread far and wide through history, the earliest written record being 100 years ago. In recent years, there have been a series of reported sightings of the monster, making it even more mysterious.

The *Annals of Changbai Mountain* claims that a man hunted deer in Changbai Mountain

in the 29th year of Emperor Guangxu's reign (1903). When he chased
the deer to the shores of Tianchi, he was suddenly terror-struck
on seeing a strange animal. It was as large as a buffalo, and its
shouts and calls resounded between heaven and earth. At
the very moment the creature threw itself on the man,
it received a shot in the belly. Screaming painfully,
it fell back into water. After a while, the lake
became shrouded in heavy fog. This is the
earliest record of the Tianchi monster.

Tianchi (Heavenly Pool) in autumn.

In *Collected Writings about Changbai Mountain*, there is a detailed record of a sighting of the monster in the second year of the reign period of Emperor Xuantong (1910) of Qing Dynasty. Four hunters had arrived at Diaobie Platform of Tianchi, and sighted a golden animal coming out of the water below Zhipan Peak. Its head was as large as an *ang* (ancient vessel with a small mouth), with a horn on its square crown, and on its long neck there was a heavy tassel. It lowered and shook its head, as if absorbing water. The hunters got scared and ran. When they were half way up the slope, they suddenly heard a loud bang. They turned to look. It disappeared. All the hunters believed it was a dragon, and thus named the lake "Dragon Pond."

The Tianchi monster was no mere legend. Since the 1960s, the number of monster sightings have kept growing. According to *Annals of Changbai Mountain*, in mid-August 1962, Zhou Fengying, from the meteorological equipment supply center of Jilin Province, saw through his binoculars two animal heads coming out of the water in the northeast corner of the lake, over 200 m away from the shore. The two heads, 200-300 m apart, were chasing each other. One moment they went down, the next they rose again. As big as the head of a dog, the two black heads created a myriad swathe of ripples on the lake, in the shape of the Chinese character "人." One hour later, the monster disappeared in the water. Another sighting happened on September 26, 1976: Lao Pu, director of a nursery in Yanji County, together with a worker and over 20 soldiers, saw a 2-m-tall creature from Tianwen Peak, resembling a buffalo, lying prostrate on the shore of Tianchi.

On August 21, 1980, a writer named Lei Jia and his friends discovered wide trumpet-like ripples on the water surface of Tianchi. He recalled, "Sometimes, a black pot-like thing emerged from the water at the pointed end of the ripples, and at other times, a shuttle-shaped body appeared, looking like the back of the monster." Just two days later, two employees of the Jilin Meteorological Bureau saw five such mysterious monsters only 30 m away in Tianchi. They said that the monsters held their heads and breasts high, with heads as big as those of oxen, bodies like dogs, and beaks like ducks. Their backs were black and shiny, covered with long brown hair, while their bellies were snow-white. The two witnesses, shouting, tried to shoot it, but missed. The monsters quickly submerged and vanished.

On July 21, 2005, Huang Xiangtong, senior engineer of the Scientific Research Institute of the Changbai Mountain Nature Reserve Administration, sighted the monster for 20 minutes and took a photo of it. The photo shows the monster had a shuttle-shaped head, and a fin on its back, the same color as the body. When its back rose out of the water, it looked just like a submarine. One moment, the monster dove down, the next it emerged from the water. More unusually, its forelimb was like a strong wing-like fin, black outside and red inside, beating the lake from time to time, raising ripples in the shape of the Chinese character "之."

Does the Tianchi monster really exist? So far, no conclusions can be drawn from the differing views. Many scientists maintain a negative attitude. They believe that the lake came into being after a volcanic eruption 290 years ago. With an annual average temperature of -7.3°C, and a frozen season lasting eight to nine months, few animals and plants would be able to survive in the lake. If there were indeed the "monsters," what would they eat? Moreover, the plesiosaur became extinct 65,000,000 years ago, so how could one appear in the lake? It is also impossible for the "monsters" to have evolved from microorganisms in the lake over such a short period of time, of about 290 years.

However, there have been more and more rumors about Tianchi monster over the past century, especially in the last 20 years. Thousands of people, Chinese and foreigners, officials and civilians, scientists and journalists, have reportedly sighted the creatures. Many have taken pictures and shot films of them. Most of the witnesses saw one "monster" in the lake, and a few saw more than two. Zhou Fengying, from the meteorological station on top of Changbai Mountain, saw the monster seven or eight times.

Witnesses give different accounts of the monster. Some said it had a small head and narrow neck, and was huge; others said it was a dragon-like creature with a horn on its square crown and many tentacles; still others said its head was as big as that of

oxen, bodies like dogs, and beaks like ducks, etc.

Photos and videos of the monster all taken or shot by the witnesses from mountaintops more than 1,000 m away the lake. Moreover, when the monster appeared, most of its body was hidden in the water. Therefore, it is still uncertain as to what kind of animal it might be.

Aiming to make a thorough investigation of the Tianchi monster and solve the world-famous mystery, the Changbai Mountain Nature Reserve Administration set up an exhibition room, collecting and displaying all the sightings and records of the monster.

There is a flow chart depicting the course of the monster coming out of the water, and two statues of it made according to the eyewitness accounts. One resembles a golden dragon, covered with scales. The other looks like an ox with a duck's beak. The non-governmental organization — Research Society of the Tianchi Monster, established in the Korean Autonomous Prefecture of Yanbian, Jilin Province, has also collected and published many materials and books about the monster, and sold souvenirs of it. Over the past few years, this organization has grown steadily, attracting members from Japan, the Democratic People's Republic of Korea and Southeast Asia.

Today, explorers, scientists and fans of the Tianchi monster from China and other countries in the world gather at Changbai Mountain. Some settle down deep in the mountain, monitoring the monster all the year round. Others keep watch day and night, braving hardships and risks.

What on earth is the Tianchi Monster? Does it really exist? This world-wide mystery will only be solved through people's unremitting efforts.

Tianchi (Heavenly Pool) in winter.

Getting Up Changbai Mountain by the Northern Road

The traditional and efficient way to get up Changbai Mountain is from the northern slope. Visitors set out from Dunhua or Yanji in Jilin Province, reach Erdao Baihe Town and start climbing the mountain the same day. On the road, visitors listen to the soughing of the wind in the forest and enjoy the beautiful scenery of lofty peaks and immense forests.

Changbai Mountain Waterfall

Between Longmen Peak and Tianhuo Peak north of Tianchi is a U-shaped gap, more than 20 m wide. It is the only natural watercourse through which water comes out of the lake. Flowing over the steep slope, the rushing river resembles an inclined scaling-ladder. It is called Tongtian River, or Chengcha River ("cha" means "raft" in Chinese). After flowing 1,250 m beyond the gap, the Chengcha River suddenly turns into churning rapids, and drops from a 68-m-high cliff. This is the famous Changbai Mountain Waterfall, the source of the Songhua River, and the largest waterfall in northeast China.

Observed from a distance, Chengcha River is like a white ribbon suspended in midair linking Tianchi with the Changbai Mountain Waterfall. It is the shortest river in the world, only 1,250 m long. Found in ancient poems, the name "Chengcha" (meaning "going by raft") was most probably given by literati. The literary allusion "going to the Milky Way on a raft" comes from *Accounts on Wide-ranging Matters*, written by Zhang Hua in the Jin Dynasty. According to the book, the Milky Way and the sea were connected. One August, a man went on a long journey on a raft filled with food. One day, he reached a place where maids were weaving cloth in a palace, and a man was watering an ox by the river. He asked the man where he had come to and learned that he had arrived on the Milky Way. When men of letters came to the source of the Songhua River, the beautiful landscape might recall to them this literary allusion, "going to the Milky Way on a raft." There is a huge stone, called the "Cowherd Ferry," standing at the outlet of the Chengcha River, which resembles a bridge, reminding visitors of the Milky Way.

▶ Changbai Mountain Waterfall.

The Cowherd Ferry divides the river into two parts. The waterfall pours down from the cliff, appearing like a white ribbon suspended in midair. Two water columns splash against the floodplain, and flow to the deep valley bottom, causing 10-m-high waves to fly in all directions, as if a goddess were strewing flowers over the earth. The place is permeated with refreshing vapors, full of power and grandeur. During mid-winter, it boasts distinctive scenery. Everything is covered by snow, but the Changbai Mountain Waterfall still courses straight down the cliff, causing drops of water to splash about, becoming frozen in the twinkling of an eye.

The most marvelous aspect of Changbai Mountain Waterfall is the image of a hoary-haired immortal, which appears between the two eastern streams of the waterfall. Formed by the specific climate conditions, the power of the wind, the volume of water and vapor, an image of an immortal, wearing his gray hair in a bun, appears in the waterfall. Following the changes in wind direction and vapor, his gray hair seems to sway. The majestic-looking immortal gazes into the distance as if lost in thought, with a long robe over his left arm, and a horsetail whisk in his right hand. He is discernible one moment, and suddenly gone the next. Sometimes, several immortals appear in the waterfall. Except on windy or rainy days, standing at different spots about 800 m away from the waterfall, visitors can see the wonder of the "Changbai Immortal" from different angles.

The magnificent Changbai Mountain Waterfall roars as if 10,000 horses were galloping forward. When passing by, visitors all stop to watch, feeling a myriad of emotions. The waterfall looks just like the Milky Way falling from the sky, but with a devastating force. Water columns flow to the bottom of the valley, where a 20-m-deep pool has taken shape after hundreds of years. Water from the pool converges into the Erdao Baihe River of Songhua River. The roaring rapids of the river whirl on and on through the valley, creating a thundering noise when they strike the rocks.

▶ Ice cascade in Changbai Mountain.

Divine Water of Changbai Mountain

Changbai Mountain is an active volcano. The last time it erupted was over 290 years ago. Though now dormant, inside it is in constant motion. As a result, hot springs well up. These hot springs have a positive therapeutic effect on many ailments, and are regarded as "Divine Water of Changbai Mountain."

There are dozens of hot spring groupings scattered on Changbai Mountain, the nearest one lying near Tianchi at the top of the mountain, and the farthest several hundreds of kilometers away. These hot spring groups vary in topography, volume of water and temperature. Hubin Hot Springs are located below Tianwen Peak at high altitude by Tianchi, with a temperature of only 32°C. Below Jinbi Peak, lies the Luquan Hot Springs, which gush out beside a huge black rock, with a temperature of 78°C. Jinjiang Hot Springs, on the upper reaches of the Jinjiang River, with seven springs, covers an area of about 10 sq. m, with hot water and air bubbles gushing out all the year round. *Accounts of Heavenly Lake of Changbai Mountain* gives a description of the Jinjiang Hot Springs. There is a spring named "Xi Yan" (Washing Eyes) one km below the Jinjiang Hot Springs. It was documented that a huge rock towered above the Shangyuan River, from the holes of which two streams of spring water kept gushing; the water could improve eyesight. Other famous hot-spring groups include "Xianrenqiao" (Immortals' Bridge) Hot Springs and "Shiba Daogou" (18 Ditches) Hot Springs. Some of the hot springs are mixed with cold springs, the most well known being Weidong Hot Springs on the western slopes of Changbai Mountain. Jumping into the spring, unaware visitors will shiver with cold.

Julong Hot Springs are the most widely dispersed on Changbai Mountain, with the biggest volume of water and the highest temperatures, also known as the "First Spring of Changbai Mountain." It lies on the northern slopes of Changbai Mountain, about one km below the Changbai Mountain Waterfall, covering an area of over 1,000 sq. m, through which the Erdao Baihe River runs. There are dozens of springs scattered on the right bank of the Erdao Baihe River, including seven large ones. Innumerable streams of hot water gush out from the earth, just like a host of dragons shooting up water, thus the name "Julong" (gathering of dragons). Entering the hot-spring area, visitors are greeted by warm currents of air. The gurgling spring water gushes from fissures in rocks. The biggest mouth of the springs is the size of a bowl, while the smallest is as thick as a finger. The spring water is yellow and turbid, dying the surrounding stones in different colors. It is an unpredictable and magnificent scene. The hot springs vary in temperature, most of them above 60°C, with the hottest reaching 82°C. Thus, the Julong

◄ Hot-spring bath in Changbai Mountain.

Hot Springs are considered hyperthermal. By the hot springs grows a rare kind of grass, which can only live at such specific temperatures. Boasting such high temperatures, the Julong Hot Springs would be able to cook an egg. If placed into the spring water, the egg is done in 20 minutes. An egg cooked by the hot spring is called a "divine egg," and is one of the wonders of Changbai Mountain. When it is done, the yolk has already congealed while the egg white is still sticky, though the reason for this remains unknown. The "divine egg" is very delicious, tasting like mineral water.

Containing hydrogen sulfide, the spring water has dyed the surrounding rocks red or green. Thanks to the presence of many mineral elements, including hydrogen sulfide, calcium and magnesium, the water here has a good therapeutic effect on many ailments. There is a bathing pool named "Yi Shen" below the Julong Hot Springs, for people who have climbed Changbai Mountain to take a bath and savor the warm waters. Many hotels on Changbai Mountain have installed water pipes, drawing on the hot spring water. Taking a hot-spring bath after a day's visit can be most refreshing, and it is also an effective treatment for arthritis and skin diseases.

In recent years, ice-and-snow tourism has been booming in Changbai Mountain. The snow routes for cross-country and alpine skiing run across the vast virgin forests, with verdant pines and white birch lining both sides. Visitors ski and take snowmobiles, enjoying themselves. An ice arena for alpine speed-skating lies at the southern slope of Changbai Mountain, using waters from the unpolluted waterfalls and hot springs of Changbai Mountain. Nestled among hills, the ice arena boasts a natural protective screen of lush green pine forest. Gazing into the distance on sunny days, one can see snow-capped mountains gleaming brilliantly, and the Changbai Mountain Waterfall descending from heaven. Looking closer, visitors are usually most charmed by the murmuring streams, so that they almost forget to turn back. Among all these winter activities, the open-air hot-spring bath is the most wonderful. In winter, surrounded by the vast expanses of white snow, the Julong Hot Springs remain veiled in steam. There is a great deal of rime hanging on nearby trees, different from that found in Jilin City on the lower reaches of the Songhua River. It is great fun to wear a swimsuit in such cold weather to play in the hot springs.

Fusong County, known as the hometown of ginseng, has five sanatoriums catering to visitors, with abundant underground source of hot-spring water. According to experts, the water here mixes more than 60 minerals, with a good therapeutic effect on many ailments. Today, the place has become a well-known holiday resort and rest spa.

"Luxurious" Civilian Life

People in Jingyu County, Jilin Province, live a "luxurious" life, envied by those in other places. Turn on the tap in their homes, and sweet and refreshing mineral water flows out. They drink it, and also wash their faces, hands and hair with it. As a result, they have fair and delicate skin, as well as smooth and shiny hair. On the streets, food cooked with mineral water and bathrooms providing mineral water are available everywhere.

The local people's "luxurious" living is attributed to the quality mineral springs of this legendary land. Changbai Mountain features not only hot springs, but also mineral springs. A total of 47 quality mineral springs have been found in Jingyu County, gushing out a total volume of 151,000 tons of water each day.

Water is the essential component of living things. Animals and plants all depend on it to keep alive. Therefore, water is the origin of life. It is also a necessary nutritive element for humankind. Practice shows that certain types of water not only satisfy one's thirst, but also improve one's health and prolong one's life. Taking a mineral-spring bath and immersing all four limbs in this water can treat skin diseases, relieve uneasiness of the body and mind, and speed recovery of chronic ailments.

At all times and in all countries, mineral waters have been deified. Early in Ancient Rome, mineral water in some European areas was regarded as "holy water," helping to treat ailments. The use of mineral water in China to treat disease traces its history back to 3,000 years ago. With references found in ancient literature, Chinese people realized long ago that mineral water helps to maintain health and treats many ailments, including some stubborn ones. Modern scientific analysis and surveys also show that people who drink mineral water for years have lower incidences of certain diseases, including cancer, compared to those who drink other sources of water. Moreover, they have a higher growth index and a longer average lifespan. Hydrochemical analysis can prove that mineral water is unpolluted and contains a wealth of mineral substances and microelements. This is the main reason for its nutritive and therapeutic effects, which are far better than

other sources of water.

Domestic water in Jingyu County comes from the Qinglong Spring, which is directly drinkable. It is natural, unpolluted mineral water. There are also high-grade mineral springs in Baishan City in the hinterland of Changbai Mountain. To date, 130 mineral springs have been found in Baishan, with a total volume flow of 260,000 tons each day. As Baishan has a forest coverage rate of

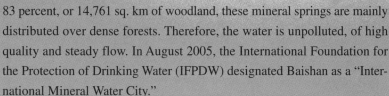

Alpine skiing.

83 percent, or 14,761 sq. km of woodland, these mineral springs are mainly distributed over dense forests. Therefore, the water is unpolluted, of high quality and steady flow. In August 2005, the International Foundation for the Protection of Drinking Water (IFPDW) designated Baishan as a "International Mineral Water City."

Fortunately, this high-grade mineral water has now also been made available to other places in China. The Jingyu Plant of Nongfu Spring Co. Ltd. is one of the few industrial scenic sights of Jilin Province. It stands in the frigid zone of the hinterland of Changbai Mountain, which is sparsely populated and covered with dense forest. Owing to the Changbai volcano groups of the Quaternary Period, the water has become rich in mineral content over a prolonged geological period. The Nongfu Spring subsidiary in Jingyu County bottles water from a spring called "Cuocao Spring," with an outflow of 35,000 tons a day. A national-standard "mineral water nature reserve" was established at the site, which has no human habitation for 10 sq. km surrounding it. The workshops, constructed to international standards, are situated in the beautiful forest. It is clearly an environmental-friendly forest factory not only in name but in reality as well. It is the best production base for mineral water in China, perfectly combining modern industry and virgin forest. In the near future, the quality mineral water of Changbai Mountain will become available all over the world.

"Beauty Pine"

Famous mountains and scenic sites are usually accompanied by beautiful pine trees, and Changbai Mountain is no exception. Take a bus to Erdao Baihe Station, or walk up along the horizontally distributed vegetation zone, and you will see extremely elegant trees on both sides of the Baihe River or in the mixed forest of coniferous and broadleaf trees. They stand gracefully tall and erect, more than 10 m high, shoulders above all other trees. This is the famed "beauty pine" of Changbai Mountain.

Beauty pine has been labeled as the top pine tree of Changbai Mountain. Its trunk is tall, straight and smooth, pale brown and pink. The lower branches usually have all fallen off. The verdant crown, in the shape of an umbrella, is composed of short and thick acerose leaves; below stretch out several graceful branches, in such smooth lines that they remind people of the missing arms of Venus de Milo.

Beauty pine is unique to Changbai Mountain, which is indeed as beautiful as its name. Since it can only grow on Changbai Mountain, it is also named "Changbai pine." Some grow scattered in the mixed forests of Korean pine, spruce-fir, coniferous and broadleaf trees, while small unbroken stretches of this pine can be found only near Erdao Baihe Town. The tree is elegant and towering, combining the straightness of pine and the grace of a woman, making it most impressive. Climbing up Changbai Mountain from the northern slope, beauty pine is the first thing that comes into view. Some stand alone like young girls in their boudoirs. Others grow side by side like a flock of beauties. Visitors become so infatuated with the tree that they are reluctant to leave.

Beauty pine has become a symbol of Changbai Mountain, like the "pine greeting guests" of the Huangshan Mountain. It is a rare tree endemic to Changbai Mountain, included on the national list of Class 2 protected plants, and is a variant type of the European red pine. Beauty pine is distributed over the Changbai Mountain Nature Reserve and the Erdao Baihe region. Its living environment is truly mystifying. Beauty pine can only survive in the infertile volcanic ash of Changbai Mountain, growing luxuriantly and suffering no insect pestilence, making it a real wonder of nature. It not only has a charming appearance, but also braves the severity of winter. The colder it is, the more verdant beauty pine seems to grow.

More interestingly, the older the beauty pine grows the more attractive it appears, contrary to humans. At an early age, the tree is nothing special. However, when it ages, it begins to look much more graceful. The ones over 100 years old are especially enchanting, combining mature elegance with a certain girlish shyness. The tallest beauty pine is about 32 m high, and over 400 years old. According to botanists, Changbai pine is an ideal variety of tree for afforestation, giving it great scientific and economic significance, to play an important role in the preservation of species and the systematic study of gymnosperm.

The Changbai Pine Nature Reserve was established in Jilin Province in 1985 to protect the gene pool of the tree. There is a management station that was specially built for the beauty pine on the reserve, costing millions of yuan to operate. Almost all the staff members are women. They cherish the beauty pine like their own sisters, establishing an archive for each one.

Huts of people living in Changbai Mountain.

Underground Forest

Tourists who wish to get some personal experience of the fantastic and precipitous peaks of Changbai Mountain are recommended to visit the "underground forest." This mysterious and vast forest can certainly fulfill the wishes of people who have long lived in the cities to return to nature and seek novelty and adventure in the unknown.

The "underground forest," also called Huokou (Volcano Mouth) Forest or Gudi (Valley Bottom) Forest, is a scenic area at the lowest altitudes in Changbai Mountain. Go upward along the road on the northern side of Changbai Mountain and through the mountain gate, you will soon come upon the entrance to the "underground forest" on the right side of the road.

To get to the "underground forest," one must first go through the "ground-level" virgin forest, which is so dense that it blocks out the sunlight. A narrow trail winds ahead into the forest. It is covered with a thick layer of moss, lichen and exposed tree roots. Sometimes, you find a thick trunk lying across the path, a tree so huge it would take several people to embrace it with outstretched arms, and you have to make your way through a gap under the trunk. Some of the trees have lain fallen so long, they are rotten inside, though their outward appearance seems nothing unusual. Yet, when you step on it, the tree suddenly crashes inwards.

Walk for a while in the forest, and you soon hear the sound of water, which leads you to the "Undercurrent Cave Waterfall," another famous setting close to the "underground forest" in the Changbai Mountain. Originating from Erdao Baihe of the Heavenly Pool (Tianchi), the waterfall cuts the hard basalt ground into two. You can stride over the underground drain in one step, and find the Cave Waterfall hidden within. Standing in the Longyin (Dragon Roaring) Pavilion on the northern bank, you will feel the huge rock underfoot shaking, listen to deafening rumbling of the waterfall. Yet, you cannot see the current.

The Chinese nation has developed a high level of cultural refinement. From time immemorial, the Chinese people have developed a sophisticated cultural concept while frequenting the landscape wonders. For example, when observing a waterfall, the highlight would be to listen to the sounds in the distance, more so than approaching too close to the waterfall. Closing their eyes, holding their breath, lowering their voice and listening with respectful attention — this is what is meant by "listening to the waterfall." It is more thrilling to hear the water rumbling down upon stone steps and dropping into the deep abyss than it is to simply look upon the waterfall; and it is more relaxing to listen to the river singing in the deep valley, among flowers, grasses and trees in the mountain and feel it inside your ears than listen to a light concert.

After walking for over half an hour, you will find yourself in a bright open space. Look into the distance, an immense forest appears at your feet, with a crown dozens of meters in height. As the wind blows, you will hear the soughing of the pines, a sound that refreshes.

The "underground forest" is in a 3-km-long deep valley, with the cliffs on both sides standing 50-60 m high. It is the haunt of beasts and people can get easily lost inside it. For the safety of tourists, the local tourism department strictly forbids tourists to go into the "underground forest" without local guides.

As you proceed, you need to cling to the cliff and walk down the natural stone steps with extreme care. On the cliffs grow exotic trees and rare grasses. Sometimes, you may come across wildlife, such as sika deer, wild boar or black bear hunting for food or drinking in the valley bottom.

In mention of "virgin forest," people usually think of huge trees growing lush and blocking out the sunlight — an awesome sight. Yet, this vast virgin forest is even more extraordinary and hazardous than usual. In the depths of the forest, it is dark, gloomy, cold and dank; numerous mushrooms grow on tree trunks; the thick layer of dry branches and fallen leaves on the ground is soft and sends forth the fragrance of humus soil, into which you sink your feet. And the fern fiddleheads, which are usually low, can grow to the height of a man here.

Trees in the "underground forest" grow densely, most being coniferous. Pine and fir tower into the sky, while huge rocks can be found scattered here and there. The Erdao Baihe River runs through the northern part of the forest. The mountain, water, rocks and forest become integrated into a whole, creating a multi-layered and splendid natural landscape.

On the left cliff along the Erdao Baihe River, you can see six ancient tree fossils arranged in a sequence, about 7-8 m horizontally, and 6 m in depth. They were formed about one million years ago. Together with the "underground forest" and Cave Waterfall, these tree fossils form a wholly unique landscape.

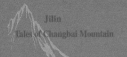
Goddess Bathing Pool

About 30.4 km northwest of Tianwen Peak in the Changbai Mountain, there is a "Round Pool" in the shape of a lotus leaf. In the Manchurian language, it is called "Belehuli," meaning "Dragon Horse." Legend has it that, long ago, on the third day of the third lunar month, when people approached the pool they had a vision of music and dance platform floating on the water surface and heard lofty music, yet they could actually see no performers but clouds and mists above the pool. After about half an hour it turned silent again. For this reason, the pool was also called "Immortal Lake."

The Qing-dynasty imperial family had always considered the "Round Pool" a sacred site and the birthplace of the Manchus. Many important historical documents record the beautiful myth of the "Round Pool" in relation to the origin of the Aisin Gioro clan, founder of the Qing Dynasty. The story goes like this: In the northeast of Changbai Mountain stands Bukuli Mountain, with a lake at its foot known as "Bulehuli." One day, three fairy maidens descended to the world, and bathed in the lake. The eldest sister was named Engulun, the second was Zhenggulun and the youngest was Fokulun. The three sisters had a fine time bathing and amusing themselves in the lake. When they went ashore to dress, an immortal magpie flew by carrying a red fruit in its beak and placed it on Fokulun's clothes. Seeing the bright-colored fruit, Fokulun was so taken with it, she held it in her mouth while putting on her clothing. However, she accidentally swallowed it, and immediately became pregnant. Thus, she could not return to the Heavenly Palace, and had to remain in the human world, to give birth to a baby, named Bukuli Yongshun. The boy could speak as soon as he was born, grew in the wind, and soon became an adult. Fokulun told him the story of his birth and his family name, "Aisin Gioro." Bukuli Yongshun turned out to be the forerunner of the Manchus. In 1908, the 34th year of the Guangxu reign period of the Qing Dynasty, Liu Jianfeng, candidate for county magistrate in Fengtian (Liaoning Province nowadays), searching for the ancestral line of the Manchu imperial family, arrived at this spot. To commemorate the ancestor of the Qing imperial court, he set up a stone tablet there, renaming the pool "Tiannü Yugong Chi" (Goddess Bathing Pool) for people to pay their respects. Hence, the pool acquired its new name.

The Goddess Bathing Pool is a small volcanic lake. Clear and shallow, it has many water plants. The center of the lake does neither freeze in winter nor has duckweed in summer. No water flows into it, nor does the lake overflow, although a spring in the pool gushes out. Around the lake are tall pines and lush green grass. Swifts soar above, fish swim at the shallow bottom, and white cranes frolic with each other. All these images evoke a paradise in the human world.

Changbai Mountain is the birthplace of the Manchus and also of the Manchu culture. Formerly referred to as the "Nüzhens," the Manchus are an ancient people from Changbai Mountain. After unifying China, the Qing imperial court abolished their old name "Nüzhen" and decided to call northeast China where they live "Manzhou (Manchuria)," and named themselves Manchus after the Revolution of 1911. The Manchu people believe in ancient shamanism and hold that all creatures have souls, taking everything on the Changbai Mountain as an incarnation of an immortal. Many aspects of the Manchu culture and a lot of their customs are closely related to the mountain, as constantly evidenced in one of the most famous Chinese classic novels *Dream of the Red Mansions* by the Manchu writer Cao Xueqin. The contents of this world-famous literary classic, from the myth at the very outset to the details inside, from offerings to ancestors to extant customs, from religious faith to dress and adornments, all have innumerable links with the Changbai Mountain. Pictured on the left is a facial makeup used in shamanism. Pictured above are Manchu girls in Manchu attire.

Located to the southeast of Lishu County in Siping, the ancient city of Yehenala is a scenic site famous for its folk customs, as well as its ancient castles in the Nüzhen style. In the late Yuan and early Ming dynasties, the forefathers of the Yehe clan conquered the weaker tribes in neighboring areas, and then had two castles built on top of strategically important mountain peaks along the Yehe River for easy defense. In early 1619, the Yehe clan was wiped out by Nurhachi (1559-1626), the posthumous Emperor Taizu of the Qing Dynasty. The Yehe clan was one of the birthplaces of the Manchus and is closely related to the imperial clan of the Qing Dynasty. Empress Xiaoci, wife of Nurhachi, and Empress Dowager Cixi (1835-1908) were both born in Yehenala, which is thus known "home to two empresses." Now, the hospitable Yehe people still maintain certain traditional Manchu culture and customs. They greet all Chinese and overseas tourists with unique Manchu etiquettes.

▶ The Goddess Bathing Pool.

The Poetic and Picturesque Western Slope

It is wiser to climb up the Changbai Mountain from the western slope, since given its distinctive wonders, it preserves a comprehensive primeval view of the mountain.

Reaching the North Pole in Half a Day

"Come to Changbai Mountain, and you can reach the North Pole in half a day." The highest peak of the Changbai Mountain is 2,691 m above sea level. Climbing up it from the western foot, the distance to its highest point is less than 100 km, but with the altitude rising by 2,000 m. Without veering off on the way to the summit, you may have a look of four vertical zones of scenery with vegetation ranging from what is typical for the North Temperate Zone to the North Pole. Such a landscape is rare for big mountains in the Northern Hemisphere.

The first view, from 500 m to 1,100 m above sea level, is of a mixed belt of coniferous and broad-leaved forests. This forest area flourishes with a range of vegetation, both in variety and in structure. The vegetation from the top to the bottom may be categorized into three layers: arbors, shrubs and herbs. The representative arbor is Korean pine, one of the most precious kinds of arbor, featuring a height of almost 30 to 40 m, a straight trunk, and timber of fine quality and wide usage. Korean pine is a neutral kind of tree, with its early growth requiring a shaded environment. Besides Korean pine, there are other arbors, such as *Larix olgensis*, *Picea jezoensis*, *Pinus sylvestriformis*, and a few ground hemlock broad-leaved trees include *Ulmus davidiana*, *Quercus mongolica*, *Fraxinus mandshurica*, *Juglans mandshurica*, *Populus davidiana*, birch and *Populus ussuriensis*. This forest belt also abounds in shrubs, such as *Corylus mandshurica*, *Acanthopanax gracilistylus*, *Acanthopanax senticosus*, *Celastraceous Flora*, *Flos lonicerae*, *Sambucus williamsii Hance*, *Rosaceae Rubus* and *Rosa multiflora*. Herbs in this grouping of forest are more exuberant, often forming small patches of valuable shrub groupings, of which some are more than 1 m tall, while others are only 10 cm. The shrubs most often seen are *Stramonium*, *Dryopteris crassirhizoma*, *Equisetum*, *Pteridium aquilinum*, *Adiantum pedatum* and *Carex planiculmis*. The place also abounds in liana, mainly including Amur grape vines, Actinidia kollmikta, Actinidia arguta, Akebia quinata and shizandra berry. They often twine around the shrubs and arbors, giving rise to a subtropical scenery. Old and lofty trees as well as entwined bush and liana, multifarious in name and shape, thus form a beautiful scene in this vegetation complex, with conifer and broadleaves combining together. It is because of such myriads of flourishing plant life that wildlife also roam about, such as the world-renowned Siberian tiger, rare spotted deer, mandarin duck (symbolizing friendship and love), Chinese merganser (a unique bird in China), and the highly prized *Rana chensinensis*. The place is also a habitat of wildlife such as red deer, snakes and other birds.

► Primeval Forests in Changbai Mountain.

▲ Chinese Merganser.

◀ Rana chensinensis.

▶ Rhodiola sachalinensis.

Between 1,100 m to 1,800 m above sea level lies a zone of coniferous forest, which in winter is icy cold with heavy snowfall, and in summer, warm, humid yet cool. The plants in the zone consist mainly of conifers, such as Korean pine, spruce, fir and larch, while broadleaves sparsely dot the undergrowth. The entire coniferous forest belt may be divided into two sub-zones. The medium lower area with trees, mainly Korean pines and larches, having tall trunks, wide branches and good sunlight filtering, is called the bright coniferous sub-zone. Beyond 1,600 m above sea level, Korean pines disappear, while spruce and fir are found everywhere. The higher area with trees (at a relatively higher density, where such spruce and fir grow thick, blocking the penetration of sunlight) is called the dark coniferous sub-zone. Due to the cold and moist climate, there are frequently floating cloud and fog, resulting high humidity that is good for the growth of moss, though shrubs and herbs underneath are rather thin and fragile. On the ground, mosses grow up to more than 10 cm, and there are numerous usneas hanging down from the middle and lower parts of tree canopies, as well as floating in the wind. People

Betula ermanii in Changbai Mountain.

Wild Siberian Tiger in Changbai Mountain.

call this setting, "a world of mosses." There also grows a type of herbal plant called "*Daphne koreana*," which looks ordinary, but produces extraordinary seeds. Each of its seeds, though as small as a grain of sorghum, contains tremendous heat. Eat one and you will feel like you have caught a fever. Eat two and you could hardly have a good sleep at night because of the heat the seed contains. Hence, the seeds became cold-resistant treasures for people living and working in icy cold areas. In this coniferous forest zone few animals are found, and those surviving there are all species able to resist the cold and feed on relatively singular food sources. They include rare sables, three-toed woodpeckers and *Ficedula mugimaki*.

Between 1,800 m and 2,000 m above sea level is the sub-alpine *Betula ermanii* zone, appearing like an irregular mountain skirt, surrounding the lower part of the volcanic cones of Changbai Mountain. The steep terrain, low temperature, plentiful rainfall, high humidity and strong winds mean ordinary trees are unable to survive there. Even pines, believed to be able to resist cold, wind and snow, are not found here. Only *Betula ermanii*, which people normally take no notice of, can survive and form a pure forest cover. Though the roots of the *Betula ermanii* grow well, they are low, short, bending and even creeping. Higher the elevations, the more bent and creeping they are, evolved through long endurance and adaptation to strong wind. The *Betula ermanii* at its tallest is only 10 m. The trunks of *Betula ermanii* at the higher altitude are less than one m tall.

The *Betula ermanii* zone is a special combination of alpine tundra and forest

elements, which become integrated with each other in this transitional zone. In this zone, trees are sparsely distributed, allowing in ample sunlight. As a result, shrubs and herbs grow well, with large patches seemingly inlaid between trees. The major shrub species here is *Rhododendron aureum*, what people call "ox-hide camellia." Its leaves do not fall in winter and it blossoms in early June each year, despite the wind and snow when Tianchi Lake is still frozen and the mountain slopes are still covered with snow. This kind of *Rhododendron lapponicum* grows at the peak or highest points above sea level, but blossoms extremely early, giving a peculiar colored hue to the mountainside. In this zone, no fixed animal species are found. In summer, owing to the comfortable coolness, many large animals go there to have a "vacation." To escape the scorching summer heat and unbearable bites of mosquitoes and gadflies, many animals, like red deer, boar, roe deer and bear, often migrate there to enjoy their "summer holidays."

Above the *Betula ermanii* forest, i.e. the middle upper part of the volcanic cone, is an endless alpine tundra zone, vegetation typical in the North Pole. Standing more than 2,000 m above sea level, the climatic conditions are the most severe, with almost no fully sunny days and with winds blowing nearly every day. Even in usually hot July, the highest mean temperature is 7 degrees Centigrade, and the wind above Level 6 blows for over 270 days a year. Severe natural conditions

Sea-like forest in white snow.

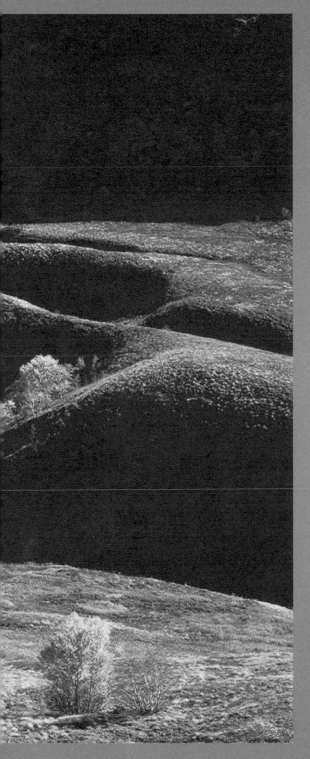

have made tall arbors disappear in this zone, leaving it with only short shrubs, perennial herbs, lichen and moss on the ground. As a result, an enormous tundra blanket has developed, formed by short plants, usually only 4 cm to 20 cm tall. In addition, the higher one goes, the shorter the plants become, and the lesser the variety. Beyond 2,600 m above sea level, almost no grasses can stay alive; only such herbs as *Oxytropis anertii* and *Rhodiola angusta Nakai* can grow weakly. Partially denuded areas often have large pieces of fallen mosses, forming a mossy mattress 10 to 15 cm deep. Despite the severe climate, however, alpine plants of various kinds struggle to live in their own special ways. Moreover, due to strong solar radiation, flowers on the high mountain top seem imbued with more vivid colors. June and July is the blossoming season in the tundra zone. Various kinds of wild flowers blaze with color. They shine against the remaining snow and wide expanse of sky, as if a large flower garden was situated at the top of the high mountain, or as if a beautiful garland surrounded the tops of clustering peaks. Animal species are few and unusual. In terms of beasts, only alpine hare is found living there. With the arrival of winter, they hibernate in small caves; while in summer they turn extraordinarily active and always run to the cave openings, romping and squeaking. Swarms of *Apuspacificus pacificus* circle the sky, their rapid flight causing the air to rustle. *Prunella collaris*, which haunts the tundra shrubbery, also comes to breed here each summer.

The Tundra physiognomy of Changbai Mountain.

65

Tizi River

In the Changbai Mountain, there is a river called the "Tizi." Judging by this unusual name, we can imagine its unique character.

To the west of the Tianchi Lake in the Changbai Mountain lies a large fault zone, which extends over 10 km from Tiyun Peak, blocking the pass up the mountainside toward the summit. The fault zone is no other but the Tizi River, which is a deep crevice formed by the strong quakes generated by volcanic eruptions. Because its course is steep, falling in stages from the top to the bottom, the Tizi River resembles alternately falling rungs, with the top ones narrower and the bottom wider, like of a house ladder, from which the Tizi River derives its name. The river is peculiar in that, if we refer to it as an above-ground river, it hides underneath the ground, with only the rumbling sound of rushing water to be heard. Thus, it has acquired other names such as "underground river" and "Yi Xian Tian" (One-Thread Sky). Yet, if we were to call it a subterranean river, its rapid torrents, however, can be clearly seen when you push aside the couch grass.

The course of the Tizi River is very narrow. At the narrowest place, you can cross it in a single step, while the widest section is no more than 3 m. So, people use logs to build "bridges" for convenient transport. Such bridges, only one or two meters long, are probably the shortest in the world.

The Tizi River, though narrow, is deep, with an average depth of about 10 m, with the deepest reaching down over 30 m. Standing on a bridge or the bank, if you position your head carefully, you can see the steep and narrow valley, with damp and smooth lichens on both sides. The water in the valley is green. It twists around, appearing then disappearing. Standing on the riverside, you can feel its comforting coolness. Standing next to the steep cliffs and rapid torrents may be rather frightening. If you drop a stone downward, it takes a long while to hear its echo.

The Tizi River has another name, "game river," since people often pick up dead animals from the river. With pieces of timber fallen in and vines spreading over the river, unless they are careful, it is hard to see the way distinctly. Therefore, wildlife, such as black bear, wild deer, roe deer and hare, easily fall into the river and are killed while migrating and dashing about.

The greatest feature of the Tizi River is that, whenever you find a dead animal, its meat remains quite fresh. This is because the river is located in an icy cold area and the frozen river only begins to melt in late June each year, with icicles hanging and a watery mist diffusing over the valley. It starts to freeze in late September, so the frost-free period is only three months. The water temperature is low, with the highest temperature only 3 to 4 degrees Centigrade. Frontier guards stationed nearby regard the river as a natural refrigerator. When fish, meat and vegetables are transported up from the foot of the mountain, they are hung sunk into the river for storage. These things can be taken at any time, and freshness is guaranteed.

▶ A mountain stream.

The Great Gorge of Changbai Mountain

In July 1987, Changbai Mountain endured a windstorm, during which its forests were severely damaged. Thousands of hectares of forests were damaged to varying extents. After the storm, a Changbai Mountain research team arrived at the disaster-stricken spot. While investigating the damage caused to the forests, they happened upon a barely known great gorge, later considered to be the "Great Gorge of Changbai Mountain," another natural wonder in Jilin Province.

The great gorge, located on the western slopes of Changbai Mountain, turns out to be a fault zone formed during volcanic eruptions, and the upper source of the Jinjiang River. The northern Jinjiang River flows in the valley of the gorge. Thus, it is also known as the "Great Gorge of Jinjiang River." The great gorge is about 60 km long, over 300 m at its widest, only a few meters at its narrowest, and about 150 m in vertical depth. A thick forest grows along the two banks of the gorge, with the trees standing straight and massive. Its low temperature and low humidity have resulted in the forest being covered with numerous hanging white hair. Mosses and mushrooms quietly daub their colors throughout the forest.

◀ The Great Gorge of Changbai Mountain.

The scenery of the great gorge that elicits the most admiration is the lava-cast forest found along the two sides of it. The lava-cast forest, appearing either singly or in groups, stands in the middle of the forest, with countless shapes and forms modeled into a scenic whole. Some resemble the moon; some, roosters, still some camels; there are even ones resembling a Bodhisattva, a girl embracing her lover and a mother holding her baby to her bosom. One can see how nature's prodigious craftsmanship has nourished the human imagination.

Moreover, the lava-cast forest boasts a changeful beauty. From different perspectives, one peak can miraculously present several different views. Seen from the front, it is a heavenly horse stretching its neck and letting out a long neigh; examined from the side, it is a camel in the desert; while looked from another angle, it becomes a dragon-boat in a race. The lava-cast forest looks not only like stone but also like earth. The lava forest appears solid, yet pieces can be broken off with hand; it seems soft, but has stood firm against wind and rain for hundreds of years.

The Great Gorge of Changbai Mountain is also called a "valley of love," for it is said to be a place where fairies went courting. It is also said to be a place where the Eight Immortals (in Chinese mythology) lived, where cave abodes were set up, with such names as "Divine Light,"

"Bliss," "Merit and Virtue." Other settings include "Celestials' Platform," "Commander's Tent," "Council Hall," "Affection-mirroring Rock," etc. All these names arise without doubt from legends and human imagination. Yet, they do add a mystical hue to the Great Gorge of Changbai Mountai.

The research team mentioned above also discovered many strange prints at the bottom of the valley and on its cliffs. Among these prints, the most mysterious is a line of character-like footprints engraved evenly on the rocks. Although they are said to be footprints, it is doubtful they are human, because each footprint is about one meter in size. Were these prints left by extraterrestrial beings? Or are they traces left by a savage species or the "hairy man" of Changbai Mountain, according to ancient records? Or are they remains of archaic ruins from high antiquity? To date, this remains a difficult riddle to solve.

Anyway, the Great Gorge of Changbai Mountain is endowed with mystery. We believe that each explorer or tourist will gain rich rewards from it. A new world of ideas may be opened up in the behavior and language presented by these rocks, and in this legendary and still not fully explored place under the protection of such forests.

One Buddha as Three Mountains, and Three Mountains Form One Buddha

The grandest topographical feature of Changbai Mountain is no less than the 16 fantastic peaks surrounding the Tianchi Lake. Formed by volcanic eruptions, these peaks take on various forms, such as a skyscraping pagoda, an eagle spreading its wings ready to fly, an immortal riding a crane, a girl dressing in front of her mirror, a fierce lion in a remote mountain, two wise elders playing chess, and an old snow man. It may be said that each peak is fantastic and awe-inspiring. Yet, who could ever imagine that on top of the summits can be seen the enormous " Reclining Buddha."

Standing at the turn-off of the road leading to the great gorge and look in the direction of the highest peak, under blue sky and white clouds and set off against green trees and blossoming flowers, a naturally formed figure of "Reclining Buddha," shaped by several peaks linked together, is vividly displayed before you.

The "Reclining Buddha," located to the southwest of the Tianchi Lake, is formed by three of the 16 fantastic peaks around the lake. Tiyun Peak, 2,543 m above sea level, is regarded as the head of the "Reclining Buddha." Its cliffs are steep and extend up like a ladder to the sky. As the peaks undulate up and down like a ladder, the head of the "Reclining Buddha" appears resting peacefully on the Tiyun Peak, with well-proportioned forehead, eyebrows, nose and neck, and a tranquil face. Wohu Peak to the south resembles the body of the "Reclining Buddha," extending southward and displaying the Buddha's great power. To the north of the head of the "Reclining Buddha," Guanmian Peak serves as his crown. It is said that when people named it "Guanmian," the "Reclining Buddha" had not yet been discovered. Guanmian Peak had acquired its name because it appears like a royal crown.

It is said that "Giant Buddha"in Leshan, Sichuan Province, is "One Buddha as One Mountain and One Mountain Forms One Buddha," which certainly evokes admiration. But, it was chiseled out by human hands out of the mountainside. The "Reclining Buddha" in the Changbai Mountain was formed by nature. Indeed, "one Buddha stretches three mountains, and three mountains form one Buddha," compelling people to admire the power of nature. Lying high above the Tianchi Lake and even above the other peaks, the "Reclining Buddha" faces up towards blue sky and auspicious white clouds, with flowers spread all over his body. He has taken on a vivid tranquil image in repose, shining in the same hue with the other mountain peaks and limpid water in the Tianchi Lake.

Once in Changbai Mountain, you can observe the giant "Reclining Buddha" at any place from which the highest peak of the mountain can be seen. However, its image and demeanor differ depending on variations in perspective and distance. Particularly, the higher you walk up the mountain and the closer you approach it, the better look you have of the gigantic figure of the "Reclining Buddha" and his compassionate face.

The weather in Changbai Mountain is pretty changeable. In spring and summer, one minute the sun is shining and then the next it is raining; and in autumn and winter, it is sometimes clear and at other times it snows. Even if it is rainy, or the face of the "Reclining Buddha" is blanketed in cloud and mist, it does not matter. It is said that, if you observe the Buddha with devout reverence and patience, the clouds would soon scatter and the mist would soon disperse, thus the mysterious "Reclining Buddha" will present itself or part of itself for you to see. Observing the Buddha in misty weather not only allows people to have a look of his face and fulfill their wish to form a connection with the Buddha, but also produce in their minds a general sense of Buddhism.

Crossing Tizi River and walking toward Jinjiang Falls, you will be able to view the grand "Reclining Buddha" from a short distance. When you get to the ridge from which Jinjiang Falls can be seen, you can turn around and look up to the huge Buddha. Looking ahead into the distance, you will see a cliff opposite the gorge where Jinjiang Falls, straight and steep, as if cut by knife and axe. On the cliff in the shade of trees is a large cave called "Xiaodongtian."

There were few signs of human habitation on Changbai Mountain in the early 20th century because the Qing imperial court had sealed the mountain for more than two centuries. Forests have since grown thick, giving a primeval look, turning into a natural park for wildlife, such as roes, deer and bears as well as various kinds of birds. Under these circumstances, three monks suddenly appeared in Changbai Mountain and their names were Shoulü, Shouchan and Shoumi. It was said that the three men had been imperial guards in the palace of Beijing, who had become disenchanted with the Qing government's traitorous practices in front of foreign powers, and forced to become fugitives after killing some foreigners. In order to avoid arrest, they were tonsured to become monks, moving from place to place until they eventually arrived at Xiaodongtian, close to the Jinjiang hot spring on the western slope of the mountain and surrounded by trees such as pine and *Betula ermanii*. Also known as the "western garden," the area around Xiaodongtian abounds in alpine flowers in addition to exuberant *Boschniakia rossica*. Xiaodongtian is a natural

cave hidden in a forest of towering trees, making it difficult to be found. Inside, the cave is narrow, deep and spacious, suitable for human beings to live in. When the outside is a world of ice and snow, inside it is as warm as spring, with a hot spring gushing out hot water.

The three monks devoted themselves to self-cultivation and Chinese *gongfu* (martial arts) on Changbai Mountain. Among them, Shoulü stayed there until he died. He once wrote a Buddhist verse, which reads:

At the source of Jinjiang gorge causalities arise from other causes,
Tianchi Lake and waterfalls are surrounded by beautiful alpine gardens.
He, with fingers pointing towards the pines, poses as if on Buddha's seat for enlightenment,
In the cave Shoulü meditated to attain the Buddhist law.
All beings who are saved help to produce a world of bliss,
In dire times of despair, as a hermit in Xiaodongtian he had left the secular world.

Level 2 of Jinjiang Falls, with a total drop of 70 m, is found at the start of the Great Gorge of Changbai Mountain. Between Jinjiang Falls, whose waves can be heard five km away, and Tianchi Lake, is the large alpine garden of Changbai Mountain, with blossoming flowers all over the mountain. "Xiaodongtian" mentioned in the verse refers to this natural cave. At that time, Monk Shoulü, who either stood at the opening of the cave or sat inside it, could see the "Reclining Buddha." Since the three monks entered the mountain, there had been no news of them whatsoever. Many who revered the Buddha as well as secular people went searching for Shoulü. Later, people found the Buddhist verse and began to search around the Jinjiang Falls. It is since then they started to form a connection with the "Reclining Buddha." On July 28, 1996, people eventually found in Xiaodongtian cave the bones of Monk Shoulü, solving the enigma that had puzzled people for nearly 100 years.

The "Reclining Buddha" lies stretched across Changbai Mountain. Owing to the seasonal climate, you might not see it every day. Only after the ice and snow have melted and the sun is shining, with the cloud and fog vanishing, is it possible to have a good look at it. Therefore, when strangers come to visit Changbai Mountain, not all of them see the "Reclining Buddha." However, Changbai Mountain, famous for its desolation, antiquity, grandeur, wonder and mystery, has established a connection with the Buddha. In recent years, some scenic views related to the Buddha have been discovered in Changbai Mountain.

On the southern slope of Changbai Mountain and in Ji'an City, which is located by the Yalu River, "Suspended Buddha" has been discovered. Over Wunü (Five-Girl) Peak are two precipitous rocky peaks over 20 m tall, between which is a crevice of equal width. Standing below in the middle of the two peaks and looking up, you can see the "Suspended Buddha" hanging right across the sky between the cliffs: the two elliptic granite stones between the cliffs form the head and body. The "Suspended Buddha" has clear features with eyes as well as teeth taking on a

natural white color, and the wrinkles on the nose easily identifiable. Its vivid expression seems to come out from between the cliffs, gazing at those who pass through below.

In Bao'an Village, Lafa Town, Jiaohe City, there is a range, a branch of Changbai Mountain, called "Shanzuishan," which forms another tremendous "Reclining Buddha" stretching several kilometers. If you look at the "Reclining Buddha" from the 324 km marker of the Tumen-Ulan Hot Highway, you can see its form rendered to perfection, as if it were a work of art done by supernatural beings. The "Reclining Buddha" lies on his back between heaven and earth with his head to the northwest and feet to the southeast. It presents an image of a man of great insight, deep in thought. His hair is thick and curled. His five sense organs are clear and vivid: eyes subtly reveal rays of light, nose well proportioned with its tip rising slightly, clear-cut contours appearing between the two lips. The two lips are fat, with the lower slightly buttressing the upper, and seem in a half-open state. The most impressive thing is that the chin is slightly sunken, appearing so real. The chest is fleshy. The outline of abdomen and legs are clear, knees between thigh and calf being distinct. The feet are bulging. The right arm is placed naturally along the sides of the chest and abdomen. The right hand is placed below the lower abdomen. Known as the "Bao'an Reclining Buddha," it is one of the eight "Reclining Buddha's" found in China. This fantastic natural wonder was listed as one of 12 natural wonders in China.

The phenomena of "Buddha's Halo" can also be found in Changbai Mountain. On January 7, 1991, Gao Ling, a journalist from *Chinese Journal of Aeronautics*, along with others, discovered "Buddha's Halo" while they were looking at Tianchi Lake from the summit of Changbai Mountain. In the thin fog above Tianchi Lake there appeared two or three rainbow-like arcs of color, in the middle of which emerged a humanlike black shadow with its arms moving. This phenomenon lasted for 40 minutes. In July the same year, a man named Qing Huiming observed "Buddha's Halo" again by Tianchi Lake. A few minutes after six that morning, the sun had been covered by white clouds. Suddenly, between the summit of the mountain and Tianchi Lake appeared a color mass, which spread in all directions, forming beautiful arc of color, in the middle of which stood a human shadow. "Buddha's Halo" followed the movement of the shadow to the left or the right, and lasted for about three minutes, weakening gradually until it disappeared as the sunlight became stronger. Both occurrences of "Buddha's Halo" were photographed.

According to scientists, "Buddha's Halo," like a mirage, is an unusual optical illusion. When a visitor stands at the mountain summit with his or her back to the sun, with clouds and fog filling the sky in front below, in the lower front direction one may sometimes see bright color rings, purple inside and red outside. In the middle appears the shadow of the viewer. The shadow follows the viewer's movements, with the ring becoming empty when the viewer moves away. The strangest thing is that, even if two people stand shoulder by shoulder, what is seen is only the shadow of the viewer.

Autumn on Laohubei in Changbai Mountain. Laohubei is a natural wonder on the western slopes of Changbai Mountain. Laohubei, literally meaning "the back of tiger" resembles a lying tiger, on which footpaths meander. The most beautiful season on Laohubei is autumn, when the tundra zone, mainly red, presents a fantastic natural wonder. This vision lasts for only several days.

"Union of Pine and Birch"

On the vast blanket-like grasslands of the western slopes of Changbai Mountain, we often see the moving scene of pine and birch standing together. The pines, tall and straight, in their serene surroundings, resemble virile men; while the birches, lithe and pretty, with outstretched branches and leaves, seem like gentle and charming beauties. They are likened to lovers courting on Changbai Mountain, known as the "union of pine and birch."

The "union of pine and birch" is excellent scenery exclusive to Changbai Mountain, not to be found in any other great mountains or rivers. This wonderful scenery is situated in the "alpine garden" zone about 2,000 m above sea level, where the coniferous forests and *Betula ermanii* forests mesh. Pine and birch, the representative plants belonging to the two respective vegetation belts, are seen snuggling up to each other like infatuated lovers, with their roots and branches interlaced and growing together. Such a phenomenon of two different tree varieties growing and joining with each other is seen in many places. Yet, the "union of pine and birch" differs in that the two trees take on different appearances, yet grow in clusters and buttress each other.

During different seasons, the "union of pine and birth" takes on different vistas. In spring, new leaves of pine and birch appear, like pairs of boys and girls experiencing first love, exuding tenderness and adoration. In summer, they thrive under a green canopy, like ardent lovers. In autumn, birch leaves can be seen experiencing early frost,

Betula ermanii on Changbai Mountain.

with pinecones hanging in clusters; the trees resemble middle-aged couples going through enduring and deepened love, helping and comforting each other. In winter, the birch stands against the wind, while the green pine braves the snow; they support each other hand in hand, recalling all the changes over the course of time.

Of the phenomenon of "union of pine and birch," there is one especially eye-catching pair, both over 300 years old. The pine is over 20 m tall, and the birch slightly shorter. They are called "King and Queen of 'Pine-Birch Unions'," also known as "Husband-and-Wife Trees."

It is because of such peculiar trees that a profoundly heart-wrenching legend has circulated among the locals of Changbai Mountain, evoking the charm of the culture of this mountain region. It is said that 300 years ago, two lovers from childhood, the boy Wang Song and the girl Li Hua, made a living by hunting and gathering ginseng. They loved each other sincerely and deeply, and both worked hard and were brave. Whenever anyone in the neighborhood had trouble, they would do what they could to help. One day in late autumn, a neighbor advanced in age needed an aged mountain ginseng to save his life. The two young lovers decided to go into the snow-sealed mountains. As they had hoped, they found and dug up the ginseng. On their way back, they encountered a villain named Sun Tancai, who knocked Wang unconscious, and spirited Li Hua away. After Wang revived, he overcame all difficulties and finally found the place where the villain was hiding out. Wang risked his life to rescue Li and was successful. But, they were pursued into the ancient forests. The villain and his cohorts used threats together with bribes, claiming Wang and Li would be saved if Li Hua was turned over to Sun. However, Wang and Li vowed never to separate. The villain had his men camped at the foot of the mountain, waiting for the young couple to come down. The trapped young couple survived by eating wild fruits when hungry, and drinking mountain spring-water when thirsty. However, when the time came for the snowfall to seal the mountain pass, they could no longer sustain their strength and embraced each other tight unto their death. During the second spring, in the place where they had died, grew a strange tree with one stem being pine and the other being birch, sharing the same root, which later has been known as the "King and Queen of 'Pine-Birch Unions'."

How could two distinctively different varieties of trees share one root? This is the mystical part of Changbai Mountain. Botanists explain that the intergrowth of two trees are able to survive in harsh conditions, while pines or birches alone could hardly live at the summit of Changbai Mountain where the elevation is so high, the topsoil so thin, with strong winds but sufficient amount of moisture.

A typical "union of pine and birch" in Changbai Mountain. ▶

"A Stone That Floats in Water, and Wood That Sinks"

It is common knowledge, even to children, that a stone will sink in water, while wood floats. On Changbai Mountain, however, there is a type of stone that does not sink but floats in water, following the currents, like a small boat, but a kind of wood that cannot float but sinks instead.

The stone that floats is pumice, also known by the locals as "honeycomb stone" or "foam stone." According to historical records of Changbai Mountain, the pumice found on the surface of Tianchi Lake was lung-shaped, thus its name "sea-lung stone." How was this pumice formed? A legend goes like this: A long time ago, there was no water in Tianchi Lake. Fire was everywhere, filling the skies with rising smoke. There were two brothers called Yu Zhu and Tian Zhu, who heard that Changbai Mountain had become a mountain of fire with no grass. The compassionate brothers prayed to the Jade Emperor for rain. After three days and nights of rain, the fire was quenched, but it left Changbai Mountain dry, without any water. The two brothers decided to dig a well. They worked day and night until the 49th day, when suddenly a wild fire leapt out from the well. They retreated to the peak summit only to see the fire burning even wilder. In the midst of this crisis, they made a quick decision, and hurriedly filled the well with stones. After seven days and nights, the fire was put out. The two brothers went on to dig up the well, neglecting everything else. They first dug out the stones filling the well, which had been burnt and become light with honeycomb holes on the surface. After days of digging, they struck water, which overflowed quickly to the summit. Those honeycombed stones all floated away on water surface. The well was the Tianchi Lake; and the burnt stones were pumice. In reality, pumice was formed by lava erupting out of volcanoes in Tianchi Lake. All over the stones' surface are bubble holes, so full of air that it is lightweight. No matter how big a piece it is, pumice can float on water. Thus, it acquired the name "floating-stone." With a surface similar to mountain stone, the color of pumice varies from yellow, gray, brown to black. Though a piece of pumice might look big, you can easily lift it. People consider this a peculiarity of northeast China. These unusual stones can be found in the forests in a circumference of thousands of *li*. Washed down from Tianchi Lake to

Songhua River, a large amount of pumice floats along the river, passing through the mountains, the Northeast Plains, and finally to the sea via Heilongjiang River. Floating in water, the part under water is wet while the part above water is dry. When the sun shines on the dry side, small particles give off an amazing metal-like luster, creating a natural vision along the vast expanses of Songhua River.

Pumice has many uses. Local people often use it to build walls due to its portability. When it is used as grinding stone, rust can be removed easily; and when used for bathing, dirt on the feet is easily removed, too. As pumice is lightweight and non-heat conducive, it may be made into hollow brick or interior decoration face bricks to prevent against heat loss or fire. Some clothing factories buy large quantities of such stones to stonewash jeans and pants. At the foot of Changbai Mountain, pumice presents a good way for individuals and enterprises to get rich.

Wood is usually able to float in water. In light of this feature, ancient people used it for canoes and as planks for boats, being a great convenience to people in production and life. But, in Changbai Mountain, there are at least four or five types of wood that sink down to the bottom of water. At an elevation of about 1,700 m on Changbai Mountain, there grows a kind of *Betula ermanii*, which the locals call "iron tree," or "alpine birch," that is hard and has such a heavy density that it cannot float in water, but sinks to the bottom of water. The other tree varieties that live in the same zone with *Betula ermanii* do not have such qualities. The reasons remain a mystery. Discovering the uses for this kind of tree still awaits further research.

Another peculiar tree variety is *Acer mono*, which is as hard as steel, exceeding the density of water several times over. Therefore, it sinks immediately as soon as it is placed in water. Of course, this kind of tree is very rare. Without the assistance of locals or forest experts, it is difficult for ordinary people to find.

Sanjiaolongwan Falls. Also called Heilong (Black Dragon) Pond, it is hidden in high mountains and thick forests, 45 km southeast to Chaoyang Town, Huinan County. Heilong Pond was formed by seepage from the opening of an ancient volcano. Because the water surface is triangular and at the south of the lake stands a 30-m-tall triangular rock, the pond acquired its name "Sanjiaolongwan." Due to its charm, the place has become a multi-purpose tourist area integrating sightseeing, hunting, skiing, ice-skating, convalescence, as well as scientific research.

Folk Customs of Koreans on Eastern Slopes of Changbai Mountain

The Korean Autonomous Prefecture of Yanbian, located on the eastern slopes of Changbai Mountain, is the only autonomous prefecture in China mainly inhabited by Koreans as indigenous residents. Their folk customs have been passed down from generation to generation and remained alive in the hearts of all people for over thousands of years. People here regard the white color as beautiful, worship the moon, make friends through songs, and are very proud of their dances.

A Land of Song and Dance

Yanbian has always enjoyed the reputation of being "a land of song and dance" due to people's inherent genius for singing and dancing. Thus, what may be seen are fabulous dances and what may be heard are marvelous songs, when you take your first step onto the wonderland of the Korean Autonomous Prefecture of Yanbian.

It almost seems that the creator showed a preference for the people of Korean ethnic group over others in bestowing them with such original talent in singing and dancing. Singing and dancing are considered a requisite for these Korean people, just like sunshine. Usually, if only one young man improvises a dance, others will follow him, spontaneously dancing together. The whole scene is quite inspiring and energizing, and the more unisonant the song is, the louder the applause. Song and dance are liked not only by the young but also by the old, and even small infants take part. Many agricultural features may be found in their dances, since the Korean people have long been work-

ing with paddy fields. Based on ancient traditional cultures, they eventually developed an elegant and unconstrained dancing style under the particular conditions of northeast China.

The singing and dancing of the Koreans has a kind of unusual charm, especially in women's dances. Women dance lightly and gracefully, every movement putting the audience completely at ease with an unending sense of beauty. They may hold fans or tap bowls or weave ribbons while dancing. The style of their dances is sometimes light and slow, soft and supple, and other times bold and forceful. They indeed represent a perfect integration of brightness and nuance, full of precision and generosity. The most famous is the Long-Drum Dance, which has a long history. We can find mural paintings of dance performances similar to the Long-Drum

Some pictures taken of Korean dance.

Dance in the frescos of Dunhuang (Northern Wei
Dynasty: 386-534 AD). The dancer places the long
drum in front of her and taps it with her left hand, while
beating it with a drumstick with her right hand. She
dances, while beating the drum gently and gracefully.

"Seesaw Jumping" is the most popular game found
in Korean customs, especially fascinating women. A
6-m-long plank, half a meter wide, is set up as the
seesaw, and raised half a meter. Two girls stand on each
end of the plank and jump one after another. The height
they reach is about 3 or 4 m. Meanwhile, they also may
choose different poses, such as straddling, casting
garlands, playing with fans, weaving ribbons, and so
on. The eye-catching performance combines slow and
fast tempos with a light and elegant manner, just like
purple swallows flying up towards the sky. Women in
colorful skirts play "seesaw" on holidays, posing variously in the air with different rhythmic tempos. Their
colorful silk ribbons and skirts flap up and down as if
also dancing to accompany the dancers. This game was
invented in response to old customs. It is said that, in
ancient times, the girls and women of the Korean ethnic group were forbidden to be seen in public. So, they
devised this game to see the outside world over walls
of the yard by jumping on the seesaw. This game may
also be played as a competition. Sometimes, people
compete to win based on the height of the jump, other
times on the skills of figurative actions, for example, a
big rotation in the air, jumping over a garland, picking
up an apple, etc., where the winner is determined according to the difficulty of the action.

From remote antiquity, the custom of enjoying a
bright full moon has been popular among people of the
Korean ethnic group. The people genuinely believe that
if the young see the moon in a basin filled with well
water at night on the 15th day of each lunar month,
they would lead a happy life and their dreams would
come true.

◄ Long-drum dance of the Korean ethnic group.

Winter guide of Korean ethnic group.

Seesaw, a traditional game particularly liked by Korean women.

An Ethnic Group in White Clothes

Throughout history, people of the Korean ethnic group have preferred white clothes, so they enjoy a reputation as "an ethnic group in white clothes" or "an ethnic group of plain clothes." Perhaps, the reason is that they live at the foot of snowcapped Changbai Mountain. A legend has it that, a long time ago, it snowed heavily one day, and a Korean girl in white clothes came across an injured fawn at the top of Changbai Mountain. Out of compassion, she took it home to nurse and eventually cured the fawn. Later, whenever heavy snow had blocked the mountain pass, causing hard times for the Korean people, the fawn the girl had saved, in gratitude, led herds of deer to bring the people abundant food, even better than the usual. Eventually, the Korean people had come to believe that the white color would bring them good fortune, and thus regard white their auspicious color.

Actually, white clothes are a formal dress for the Koreans, much like professional Western-style clothing. They are only worn on important occasions, such as meeting important guests, and attending weddings or funerals. In everyday life, the Koreans prefer to don colorful and distinctive folk dress.

The traditional clothing of Korean males includes mainly a short coat, trousers, sleeveless jacket and a robe. The coat is short and loose, with a collar, which is not upright, with white lining sewn inside the collar to make it easy to remove for washing. The right front piece of the short coat is worn

on the inside, while the left one remains outside. They usually make a slipknot of the coat's sash, similar to a bow tie in front of the right chest. The sleeveless jacket is colorful, with various decorative designs and with pockets. The trousers are loose and flared, especially at the waist. One tightens the trousers by pulling across the waist firmly from right to left, tying it with a girdle. The design of the robe resembles the short coat, but covers the knees. Korean men prefer hats with a long brim, as men's hats often mark out different strata and social positions. The crotch and the legs of men's trousers are loose and large, corresponding with the Korean custom of sitting on the floor inside the house. They also need to roll up the trouser legs while working in the paddy fields. Ribbons are always tied to the bottoms of trouser legs and match with the robes worn when men go out. Nowadays, except for a few older men, especially those who live in rural areas, who wear such clothing, most people prefer western suits and fashionable dresses. When they wear their folk costume, they prefer to wear plain coats along with waistcoats, going with the loose trousers, looking quite comfortable.

A woman's costume mainly includes a jacket, skirt, over-garments (including robe, overcoat, etc), and a decorative "waist-sash," that prevents exposing the body and protects against cold. The Korean women's short coat is called the *zegaoli*, and the skirt is called the *qima*. Older and middle-aged women like to add a cotton or fur sleeveless jacket outside the over-garment, and put on a *chanqun*, an unusual Korean skirt, encircling the waist with the left lower part inserted into the waistband. The upper coats of young women and girls are shorter, sewn with red or purple silk designs on the cuffs, front pieces and armpits. Satin of various colors are selected to be made into long ribbons to match with the attractive long skirt yet without making it look flirtatious. This whole composition renders the women beautiful yet unconventional. There are some distinctive features in the women's skirts. Usually, the skirts are long and loose. The lower part reaches the feet, while the upper part is tied at the armpits. A short coat, with long sleeves having an elegant yet billowing band, along with a loose and graceful long skirt, form a vivid feature of traditional Korean women's clothing. The beauty of Korean folk clothing is expertly and vibrantly shown off through dance performances. The long skirt matches nicely with the elegant manner of the dance, evoking an irresistible charm. Korean women in daily life like to wear short skirts, and wear a half-meter square kerchief folded in half covering the forehead, tied at the back of the head.

Children's traditional clothing is embroidered with colorful floral patterns. They are made with exquisite precision. The sleeves of the upper coat are sewn in seven colors of satin, resembling a gorgeous rainbow. The rainbow represents brightness and beauty in the minds of the Koreans.

◄ Carrying a pot on head, a unique custom of the Korean ethnic group.

Unique Food

People of the Korean ethnic group mainly grow paddy, so rice has become their daily staple food. They like rice and have become adept at cooking it. The amount of water and the heating duration are considerable in cooking of rice. People usually use a flat-bottomed iron pan with a heavy and thick lid. This type of lid prevents leakage of steam, and keeps the rice soft and delicious when cooked. What is incredible is that they can also cook different flavors of rice in the same pan at one time. Soup is a requisite dish in daily life and the most famous one is *da jiangtang*, a type of soup made by boiling water with soy sauce, Chinese cabbage, *qiu baicai* (a type of Chinese cabbage harvested in autumn), edible seaweed (kelp), etc. It is boiled with fresh water and soy sauce instead of salt. Each family preserves their own soy sauce, a favorite condiment. Soy sauce is often used to flavor soups. Hot red pepper is not only a staple dish, but also a principal condiment. The northeast of China is abundant in soybean, and as with other ethnic groups, the Koreans really like to eat bean sprouts in winter. They think that the fast growth of the bean sprouts foretells the end of winter, and the beginning of spring.

People of the Korean ethnic group are very fastidious about food at festivals and celebrations. All dishes and pastries are decorated with slices of pepper, eggs, shallots, pine-nuts or walnuts, etc. There are innumerable special dishes for festivals including seasonally popular ones. The healing and nutrient components found in Korean dishes are salient. For example, *Shenqi bushen tang* (a type of soup made by cooking ginseng and roots of membranous milk vetch usually collected in spring) is very popular. *Shenxian lu* is a delicious hotpot dish, made by cooking together oxen tenderloin and seafood; it is a popular dish at certain festivals in winter. Walleye pollack is a requisite dish at *qingming* festival (the traditional Chinese Festival of Clearness and Brightness); people believe that eating this fish can obtain blessings from heaven for one's whole life. All festive dishes consist of cold dishes and raw vegetables with sauce, such as raw beef served with soy sauce and raw walleye pollack served with soy sauce. Other than rice, festival foods include many flavored pastries and snacks like *dagao*, a type of cake made of glutinous rice, and *lengmian*, a type of cold noodles with sauce. Besides traditional festivals, such dishes are also served at celebrations of one full year for a new-born, wedding ceremonies, or 60th birthdays when huge banquets are held. Traditional dishes for such banquets are varied, and modeled into marvelous forms, such as of birds, animals, etc.

Korean snacks are famous for their unique cooking methods, such as marinating, baking and braising. Korean dishes have become more popular than ever after the Korean TV series *Dachangjin* (*Jewel in the Palace*) was widely broadcasted in China. There are various Korean snacks, the most famous being *lengmian* (cold noodles with sauce), *dagao* (glutinous rice cake) and *kimchi* (pickled vegetable).

Lengmian, also known as *changshoumian* (longevity noodles), is made of 30-percent starch and 70-percent flour, mostly carefully selected buckwheat flour, and high-quality potato starch. First, *lengmian* needs to be cooked, and then scooped out for cooling down. The next step is simmering the beef and chicken to make a soup by adding some condiments, such as licorice root, pepper, ginger, monosodium glutamate, vinegar and sugar. People will usually add beef, apple-pear, cucumber slices, sesame and pepper. Then, a tough and chewy, yet cool and delicious food is ready to be served.

No pastries of the Korean people love more than *dagao* (glutinous rice cake) for its unique flavor. It resembles *niangao* (New Year's cake of the Han Chinese), not ground by a mill but pounded cooked glutinous rice in a mortar with a pestle, then added with sweetened bean paste and sesame for fragrance and sweetness. *Dagao* is used to entertain distinguished guests and has become a staple food at festivals, similar to dumplings for the Han Chinese.

Kimchi (pickled vegetables) is another requisite dish from winter to spring. It is made with exquisite care and enjoys a high reputation. The flavor of her kimchi is a test of any housewife's cuisine. The principal ingredients in *kimchi* include Chinese cabbage, balloon-flower root, radish, perilla leaves, *weicai* (a type of osmund fern) and kelp; and the staple condiments include salt, garlic, hot pepper, ginger and gourmet powder. Its main function is to enhance the appetite before dining.

The wines of the Korean ethnic group include rice wine brewed by homemakers, and local medicinal liquors, such as *mayi jiu* (made by soaking dried ants in liquor for medicinal benefits), *hongjingtian jiu* (dried red orpine in liquor), *bulao jiu* (certain dried herbs soaked in liquor), *lingzhi jiu* (dried glossy ganoderma, a valuable medicinal herb, in liquor), *yueju jiu* (dried cowberry in liquor), and so on. They are all very popular due to both their local flavor and medicinal value.

A clean environment is essential for proper tasting of Korean dishes. One should remove shoes upon entering the house, and climb onto the *kang* (heated brick bed) and sit down cross-legged. The fragrant wine and delicious dishes on the low table placed on the heated *kang*, all create a hospitable atmosphere for dining. Taking a sip of wine, having a taste of spicy *kimchi*, enjoying a toast during a ballad, and watching an eye-catching dance, all may serve to intoxicate the guests.

Glossy ganoderma.

An Ethnic Group Respecting the Old and Cherishing the Young

The Koreans are a people who revere etiquette, as well as respect their elders and cherish their young. People regard this custom as the most important etiquette for the family, and even for the entire society.

There are strict rules for daily dining and about the setting of the table. For instance, people usually place spoons and chopsticks to the right, the main meal on the left, bowl of soup nearby, other dishes at a subordinate place, and condiments in the middle of the table. The spoon is placed in the bowl when you eat, otherwise, if you put it on the table, the host would think you have already finished your meal. If there is a male elder in the family, they will specially set up a single table for him, and only when the elder begins to eat, do the others also eat. People of the Korean ethnic group highly respect the Confucian doctrine, so the hierarchy in daily dining is strictly ranked according to age. Grandchildren, daughter(s)-in-law of a family are definitely not allowed to have meals with the grandfather or father-in-law at the same table. The younger generation is not allowed to drink and smoke in front of their elders. If a younger member is allowed to smoke, he must not borrow a lighter or match from his elders, even with the elder's voluntary assistance, this being considered impolite behavior. When walking on the road accompanying an elderly, younger men should consciously follow behind. If a young man needs to pass an elder in an emergency, he must respectfully give an explanation to the elder. If a young man and an elder are walking towards each other on the road, he must convey his greeting first to the elder and stand to one side, letting the elder pass first. A young man should always use honorifics when talking with an elder, so should two young men of the same generation at their first meeting. A young man should greet elders in the family one by one during festivals. Then, he should visit all other families with elderly people in the village to convey their greetings. The 15th of the eighth lunar month is Elders' Day in the Korean Autonomous Prefecture of Yanbian, and on this day all elders over 60 years of age wear red flowers on the front of the chest and receive people's blessings.

The people of the Korean ethnic group regard their 60th year as a watershed in life. So when an elder reaches 60, his or her children will hold a *huajia* (60-year cycle) banquet to celebrate his or her 60th birthday. The *huajia* banquet, also known as *huanjia* banquet and *huijia* banquet, is rather ceremonious. In addition, Koreans also hold grand family banquets for 80th and 90th birthday celebrations. When the occasion comes, the elder's children will invite relatives and neighbors to the *huajia* banquet to celebrate together and express gratitude to their parents. The steps of

Picture of *huajia* banquet in a Korean family.

the celebration are as follows: the children help the elder put on a specially made new robe, and hold the banquet in the hall or the yard. The venerable elder, sitting in the center, receives birthday presents together with other elders of his or her generation in the same community. The celebration starts after sweets, fish, meat, cakes and other dishes have been prepared and placed on the table. The children, according to age and relationship, congratulate the venerable elder one by one. They may make a toast, recite a poem, or dance and sing. After these rituals, the celebration turns into a banquet. Everyone may dance or sing a song while eating the delicious food, and leave the banquet after enjoying to their hearts' content.

There is a tale regarding the *huajia* banquet. It goes like this: During the reign of the ancient Koguryo Kingdom (an ancient tribal kingdom in northeast China), the king promulgated a law. The law stipulated that all those aged over 60 must be buried immediately, whether alive or dead. A young man surnamed Jin was so filial that he would not bury his father, who was over 60 and still alive. He hid his old man to avert the burial. Later on, a powerful empire ordered three difficult conundrums to be solved by the Koguryo Kingdom. If no one could answer the conundrums, the kingdom would be wiped off. The king worried about this each day. One day, the young man, when bringing meals to his father, told him this story. His old man quickly figured out the correct answers to the three conundrums. The young man told the king his father's answers, thus aiding the king to overcome the crisis. Eventually, the king was told that it was the young man's father who had actually aided him against subjugation. The king was so moved that he ordered the repeal of the law. Instead, he inaugurated the *huajia* banquet to commemorate the wisdom of elders.

Marriage Customs

Marriage in the Korean culture before the 1920s was determined by the parents' will and matchmaker's words. Furthermore, there was rarely intermarriage with people of other ethnic groups. After the founding of the People's Republic of China in 1949, arranged marriages no longer took place, and free courtship has gradually prevailed with the development of society. Along with the advance of time, the Koreans are now also free to intermarry with people of Han and other ethnic groups.

Young men and women may establish a love relationship. Yet, before they prepare for their engagement, they have to inform their parents first for agreement. Then, the parents of a young man bring their son to the young woman's family to make an offer of marriage. If the young woman's parents refuse to meet, it means they do not agree with the marriage. If both of the parents agree to meet each other, it means the marriage is promising, and the young man and woman are allowed to listen by the side. If their parents give their consent, the young man should kowtow to the young woman's parents, and the young woman should also do the same to the young man's parents. At the same time, the young man and woman must definitely express their willingness to support their parents. With this, the marriage is presumed to be confirmed.

The bridegroom's family should present betrothal gifts to the bride's family before the wedding. Furniture, bedding and daily necessities are to be prepared by the bride's family as dowry. They are brought to the bridegroom's family on the wedding day.

When the wedding is held, the bride and bridegroom would sit bolt upright at the front of the table, accompanied by a bridesmaid. When ready, the bride's family is invited in to have a look first, followed by all other guests. The rich banquet shows the bridegroom's love to the bride, implying he will treat the bride well in future, a gesture to put the minds of the bride's parents and relatives at rest. Then, the bride and bridegroom will pour each other a cup of wine, and mutually toast each other by drinking wine from the other's cup to the encouraging shouts of the guests. After this salute, the bride, bridegroom and bridesmaid are left at the table, while the others return

to their guest seats to their joyful drinking and eating.

Whether the wedding banquet is held in the bride's or the bridegroom's family or in a restaurant, a special table must be set for the new couple alone. This table is called the *dazhuo* (large table). This is a custom inherited from traditional marriage rites. On this table all types of foods are displayed, including cakes and sweets. Of them, the most special is a whole braised rooster with a red pepper in its beak. This dish is indispensable for all wedding banquets of the Korean ethnic group, because it signifies auspiciousness. The rooster implies the happiness of the marriage, and the red pepper indicates fervent love of the bride and bridegroom and the prospect of more offspring. After the bridegroom has drunk up three cups of wine given to him by the best man, he will ask someone to pick a small bit from each dish on the table to offer his parents. This is called *dafeng songbao* (making a parcel of all foods to offer parents). Hidden in the bridegroom's rice bowl are three peeled boiled eggs, and he can only have half of the rice and eggs, with the rest being left for the bride.

When the wedding banquet is over, all the relatives of both families will pay a visit to the bridal chamber, sitting down around the bride and bridegroom. First, a representative of guests of the bride's family will say a few words to the new couple, followed by one of the host. Finally, the bride and bridegroom express in front of their elders their expectations of each other and demonstrate their resolve to endure all hardships and fulfill the responsibilities of their new life.

When a couple has been married for 60 years, they will hold a ceremony called *huihun* to celebrate, resembling the golden or silver anniversary in Western countries. When such occasion comes, the children of the old couple will prepare an abundant feast for their parents, and relatives and guests will be invited to toast their longevity and happiness in old age. Moreover, the old couple will put on new wedding robes and cruise around on a festooned vehicle. However, there are three requisite criteria for such a celebration: First, their marriage must have lasted for a full 60 years; second, it must be their first marriage; and lastly, their children must be living and have no criminal record.

◄ A unique Korean drum dance.

▼ Competing in folk games.

World Cultural Heritage:
Ruins of the Ancient Koguryo Kingdom

The sites of the ancient Koguryo Kingdom submitted to the 28th Session of World Heritage Committee, held in Suzhou, China on June 1, 2004, include the ancient kingdom's capitals, royal mausoleums as well as a number of tombs for the nobles. At the session, the committee agreed to list them as World Heritage sites, which include the Wunü Mountain City, Guonei City, Wandu Mountain City, 12 royal mausoleums, 26 tombs for the nobles, etc. They are mainly scattered in Ji'an City of Jilin Province and Huanren County of Liaoning Province.

Eastern Pyramid

Laoling Ridge, the southwest branch of the Changbai Mountain, runs across Ji'an, a city in the southernmost part of Jilin Province, dividing the city into two parts — the south and north. Serving as a natural barrier, it protects the valleys and plains south of the ridge from the chilly winds from the north. Thanks to abundant sunshine and water as well as fertile soil, this has long enjoyed the reputation of *xiao jiangnan* (miniature of areas south of the lower Yangtze) in northeast China. So, when the area south of the ridge is bathed in the warmth of spring, that in the north still snows. Precisely because of the area's plentiful produce and austere customs, the ancient Koguryo Kingdom selected it to establish its capital at the time of the Han and Tang dynasties.

In history, Koguryo was a local regime in China established by the ethnically minority Koreans. First appeared in 37 BC, it was destroyed by the Tang Dynasty in 668 AD. For nearly seven centuries, the kingdom had remained in close contact with the various dynastic courts in China's central plains by way of political, economic and cultural exchanges. These contacts help promote the birth of Koguryo culture and created a splendid ancient culture, as evidenced by the numerous historical ruins and cultural relics it left behind. Experts from UNESCO believe that the cultural artifacts of the ancient Koguryo Kingdom within the boundaries of China display all prominent regional features, and "represent an exceptional testimony to the vanished Koguryo civilization."

More than 10,000 ancient tombs are scattered on the plains around Ji'an, which are known locally and internationally as the Donggou Ancient Tombs. The tombs represent ruins from the slave society of the Koguryo Kingdom. Of them, the most striking is the well-preserved general's tomb. The tomb stands against the majestic Longshan Mountain in the north, and to its south is slope land exposed to the sun, providing a panoramic view. The whole compound is colossal and its

▼ The tomb of a general in Ji'an, pyramid in the orient.

construction magnificent, in a grand yet simple style resembling the pyramids for the Pharaohs of ancient Egypt. Hence, its reputation of "pyramid in the orient." What is most interesting is the path leading to the tomb, designed in the style of a staircase. When a visitor come to pay homage to the tomb, he or she must mount it step by step, thus leaving him or her with a majestic impression.

The general's tomb is an epitome of the supreme skill of architecture of ancient Koguryo. The tomb was built in seven strata with the finest granite. The first stratum was paved with four layers of granite slabs, the largest one being 5.7 m long, 1.12 m wide, 1.1 m thick and with a weight of 32 tons. Each of the other six strata was paved with three layers of granite slabs. The whole tomb is in square shape, with the base measuring 997 sq. m, and the top, 270 sq. m. Right in the middle of the fifth strata is a paved path leading to the tomb chamber. The tomb chamber is 5 m long and 5.5 m high. The walls were built with six layers of granite slabs, and its roof is covered with a huge singular stone slab about 50 sq. m in size and over 50 tons in weight. On the floor of the tomb chamber are placed side by side two stone sarcophaguses. Numerous granite slabs were used to build the tomb, more than 1,100 of which were used alone on the outer edges of the tomb. All the huge stone slabs were from a quarry 22 km away. No vehicles and cranes were available 1,500 years ago, and workers of the Koguryo Kingdom had to rely on using of rolling logs and placing earth under these huge slabs to move them up the mountain slope and deliver them to the construction site. The construction of the gigantic tomb fully reflects the wisdom and craftsmanship of the people of ancient Koguryo. The stone slabs used for the four sides of the top strata bear neatly aligned round apertures, and from the soil on top of the tomb are found plate tiles, eaves tiles with lotus patterns as well as other components such as iron chains. All this may serve as evidence that a pavilion-like structure must once stood on the top of the tomb; it also tallies with the funeral customs of other ethnic groups in northern China. At the rear of the general's tomb once stood in a line four much smaller auxiliary tombs. Now, only one is extant. Their architectural style is similar to that of the major tomb. They may be tombs for the general's concubines or favored subordinates.

It has been established that it is the tomb of King Changshou, the 12th king of the Koguryo Kingdom, built at the beginning of the fifth century AD, when the king mounted his throne. Unfortunately, the tomb suffered serious robbery in the last years of the reign period of Emperor Tongzhi of the Qing Dynasty. At that time, forced by natural disasters, many destitute refugees came to northeast China to make a living. Some crossed through a place named Liaotiaobian to enter the forbidden area of Changbai Mountain. They chanced upon the tombs and robbed them. Seeing the major tomb's grandiose, they may think it belonged to a general safeguarding the frontier, and thus named it *Jiangjun fen* (tomb of general), a named that has hence been used.

One major architectural feature of the capital of Koguryo Kingdom was that it has two parts, a city on the plain and another on a mountain. The original intention of this design was for flawless defense. For this reason, ancient Koguryo capital in Ji'an is known as "one capital, two cities." The

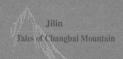
city on the plain, Guonei by name, adjoins the Yalu River to the south and stands close to the Tonggou River in the west. It was a square city built with stone, with the city walls on all sides running to 2,600 m. The highest point on the walls reaches up to four m. Ruins of the city gates, water drainage system and palaces can still be seen. Many rare relics have been found in the city. The mountain city is called Wandu. It was built on a top of a hill 2.5 km to the north. The city walls were also built with stone and run seven km in total. With the city are ruins of a watchtower, garrison barracks and palaces. The two cities are marvelously representative of all city constructions in the middle ages of northeast China. The Guonei City is a rare example of ruins, preserved on the surface, of a city built with granite on a plain, and the well-preserved city walls are really majestic and beautiful, thus making the city a historical architectural model. What is most remarkable is the construction of the city walls, all of which were built with triangular blocks of hard rock, tightly inlaid into each other, without using any sand or mud to fuse them. Despite plentiful rainfall and vastly changeable temperature in the Changbai Mountain area, the walls have stood there for over 2,000 years. Not for the remarkable technique employed, the walls would have fallen a long time ago, given the principle of expansion with heat and contraction with cold. Thanks to this unique building technique, rainwater can seep into the ground through apertures in the walls during rainy seasons. To this day, the walls of mountain cities in Eastern Asia all have followed the example of Guonei City, evidencing its profound influence in architectural art.

No. 1 Stele in the East

At the foot of a high mountain five km to the northeast of Ji'an stands the Stele of King Haotai, which boasts a reputation as the "No. 1 Stele in the East."

The Qing imperial court set up Huairen (later changed to "Huanren") County in the border region in 1877, 1,209 years after the Koguryo Kingdom disappeared. Guan Yueshen, an subordinate of the county magistrate who had been especially fascinated with epigraphy, often walked through the historical ruins in search of bronze and stone inscriptions. One day, as he was walking along the banks where the Tonggou and Yalu rivers converged, he chanced upon a stele immersed in the creeping weeds. He cleared off the lichen on the surface, checked it carefully and saw it was a stele engraved with Chinese characters. It soon proved to be the Stele of King Haotai.

In 414, Gao An, also known as King Haotai of the Koguryo Kingdom, died and was buried on the slope of Yushan Mountain by the Yalu River. Gaoan, also called Tan De, took the throne in 391 at the age of 18, and died at 39. The 20 years of the reign of King Haotai was the most prosperous period in Koguryo's history. Relying on the mighty economic and military strength of

Stele of King Haotai in Ji'an.

his kingdom, he occupied the eastern part of Liaoning, driven out Japanese pirates, took over Fuyu (present-day Fuyu County, Jilin Province) and dramatically expanded Koguryo's territory. Gaolian, his son or King Changshou, selected a huge breccias tuff and made it into a stele to record the great deeds his father had done, with the hope to make his descendants remember his father's great contribution to the kingdom. A square column colossal and darkly imposing, the stele stands on a piece of irregularly shaped granite without any extra support. Carved on its four sides are 1,775 Chinese characters in script blending the clerical and standard scripts, recording King Haotai's life achievements as well as the legendary origin and founding of the Koguryo Kingdom. The inscription is the longest, best-preserved and most valuable record of Koguryo Kingdom found to date. Since the erection of the stele, it had been paid homage by countless people of Koguryo. Yet, after the kingdom was annexed by the great Tang Empire in 668, the stele had gradually lost its former accolades and buried under a thick layer of lichen. It is until its rediscovery in 1877 that people had come to know that a thriving and flourishing kingdom once existed on this piece of fertile land.

A Treasure House of Art in Northeastern Asia

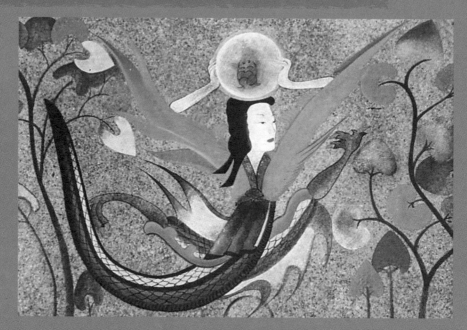

One of the most attractive and reputed aspects of the historical culture created by the people of Koguryo is found in the colorful and mysterious tomb chamber murals. Numerous, fabulous and colorful murals have been discovered in the ruins of ancient Koguryo tombs. It is said these murals appeared 300 years after the Koguryo Kingdom had been founded. They cover a wide range of subjects, and demonstrate marvelous painting technique. Although more than 1,000 years have elapsed since they were created, the murals are still vibrant and lifelike, almost like fresh artwork, indicating the painting techniques had reached quite a high level at the time.

Eulogized as "a treasure house of art in northeastern Asia," the tomb chamber murals of ancient Koguryo Kingdom serve as a record of the unique culture of ancient people in northeast China, deserving its reputation as "an enchanting flower of the 5,000-year-long Chinese civilization." According to discoveries made so far, it can be concluded that the Koguryo tomb chamber murals appeared in the early half of the 4th century AD. They not only reflect the daily lives of royal and noble families, such as banquets, singing and dancing, acrobatic performances, excursions and Buddhist worship, but also include the images of the so-called four celestial animals in the Chinese legend, i.e., vermillion bird (representing the south), black tortoise (representing the north), blue dragon (representing the east), and white tiger (representing the west). The representation of the four images were clearly products of the influence of the culture of the central plains. In terms of painting techniques, the first step was to daub lime onto the stone or brick walls, and then paint. Giving expression to the unique traditions of the Koreans, the murals include scenes of wrestling and hunting as well as images of animals found in the Changbai Mountain, such as

tiger, deer, boar, bear, roe, hare, turtledove, etc.

The Tombs of Five Helmets are graves with huge earth mounds for members of a noble family in the late period of the Koguryo Kingdom. A mixture of the cultural characteristics of Confucianism, Buddhism and Taoism, the murals in the No. 4 grave are elegant and grand, including the images of the four celestial animals, Fuxi, Nüwa. Shennong and immorals. Fuxi was a legendary ruler of the Chinese nation who taught people how to fish, hunt, and raise livestock; Nüwa was a legendary goddess in Chinese mythology, according to which she created humans and patched up the sky. And Shennong was another legendary ruler of ancient China. On the lower left corner of the north wall was painted the figure in Taoism image. He sits on a lotus throne barefooted; and his left leg is bent while the right is stretched upright. With his hair drooping, he was presented to be busy painting Eight Trigrams. The appearance of Eight Trigrams in the tomb indicates that the artist or sponsor believed that the Eight Trigrams might bless them. This distinctive Eight Trigrams was the earliest one in China, and its relation with *The Book of Changes* can be found in historical records. The culture as presented in *The Book of Changes* serves as a major source of the culture of Chinese nation, and it also serves as a prominent symbol distinguishing the Chinese culture from other cultures of the world. Therefore, the episode of "painting the Eight Trigrams" in the murals of this tomb shows the close relationship between the culture of the Koguryo Kingdom and that of the Chinese central plains.

Local departments for the preservation of cultural and historical relics have made reproductions of most of the tomb chamber murals and placed them in museums for the benefit of visitors.

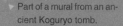
▶ Part of a mural from an ancient Koguryo tomb.

▶ Lingguang Pagoda in Changbai Mountain.

The Last Lumberjacks

The Yalu River winds its way down from Changbai Mountain southeast to Changbai County in Baishan, making this border town an idyllic place brimming with resources. About one century ago, this county was only a settlement of a few hamlets, but today, it has become a prosperous county seat. Such an incredible transformation was the result of the flowing Yalu River, and of a special group of people who lived here earlier; revered by others, they are called *muba*, meaning "team of lumberjacks."

Bygone Lumberjack Teams

Changbai Mountain is abundant in timber. The *muba* was a group of people who felled the trees and transported the lumber. They went to the mountains to cut trees in winter. When spring came, they bound them together like rafts and then set them on the river, in this way the logs were transported to other places by the river. In order to support each other, people in this trade voluntarily came together to form guilds.

The history of felling trees and rafting lumber down on rivers in the Changbai Mountain area

Silver Birch.

can be traced back to the late Yuan Dynasty (1271-1368). In 1309, the *Annals of Northeast China* recorded, "Liaoyang Branch Secretariat send people to fall trees in Changbai Mountain," and "raft-towing the lumber along the Yalu River." It can be seen that the logging trade even back then had already developed to a certain scale. However, in the following 300 years or so, the Qing Dynasty venerated Changbai Mountain as a sacred place, and claimed it as royal property reserved for the military forces, and thus the logging industry came to be strictly controlled by the imperial court. Since it was not possible for civilians to become involved, the logging trade declined.

113

In 1861, the ban on cultivating Changbai Mountain was lifted, which resulted in a wave of migration to this mountainous area. Groups of people, from places south of the Shanghaiguan Pass, rushed to the Yalu River to revive the logging trade. In the early 20th century, deforestation around the Yalu River reached its height. According to the *Annals of Changbai County*, there were over 200 lumberyards and more than 20,000 lumberjacks in Changbai County producing about 600 timber-rafts every year. Those long rafts set out from Changbai Couty and floated down the river to Dandong in Liaoning. It was the *muba* who opened the waterway linking the Changbai Mountain area to the outside world.

Lumberjack work was seasonal and divided into two types: "work on mountains" and "work on water." "Work on mountains" means felling trees, which started in the ninth lunar month to the second lunar month the next year. The lumberjacks had to live in the mountains throughout the entire winter. They set up huts, usually several dozen men in a group. They set out to fell trees before dawn. There were no holidays for the lumberjacks. Only on the eve of the Spring Festival would they give themselves half a day of rest and had a delicious meal of dumplings.

Because of sudden precipices and other dangers of mountain life, they had to be very careful. There were also many rules about tree felling. For example, to cut the first tree is called "starting a saw." Before "starting a saw," offerings were made to the mountain deity *Lao Ba Tou* (Venerable God of Lumberjacks). The first tree had to fall towards the foot of the mountain, which symbolized smooth and safe work. After felling trees, they would transport the timber down the mountain. When the mountain work was finished, a ceremony called *Qiatao* to venerate the mountain deity was conducted. The requirements for this ritual were red paper, firecrackers and a pig's head.

"Lesser Guilin" on the Yalu River.

Transporting logs down the mountain was a very dangerous job. Lumberjacks usually loaded the logs onto a cattle-drawn sledges to bring them down to the foot of the mountain. Another quick way was to let the logs roll down by themselves on an ice-covered road along a natural gully. This was called *choulinzi*, simple but very dangerous because any moment the logs may veer off the track, easily causing accidents. Many lumberjacks died beside the icy roads of Changbai Mountain.

When spring came, it brought the work on the mountain to and end. By the time, all the logs would be piled up alongside the river, and the "work on water" would begin. First job was to bundle the logs into rafts. At that time, the lumberjacks used special tools to drill holes through the logs and then bound them together with rattan to form 60-70-m-long log-rafts. When spring had initially arrived, the river water would still be freezing cold, and lumberjacks often suffered chilblains. When the rafts were made, they would start the long journey of floating down the rafts. The head lumberjack, called *toudiao*, would have to know every detail of the habits and rules of the guilds, especially about direction of the wind, the current and weather, possessing years of experience.

In the old time, the *muba* transported logs down two primary waterways:

the Yalu and Songhua rivers, commonly known as the "south and north courses."
The south course starts from the Lenggouzi in Changbai County to Shahekou
in Lao'andong (Dandong in Liaoning Province today), with a total distance of
790 km. Usually, it would take two or three months for one trip. Under no
circumstances could they be slack or slow down. If it became stormy, only then
would they stop the rafts on the banks. Only during such emergency conditions
would they rest a while, smoking and chatting. When the weather improved,
they would have to hurry on again. Today, you can still see deep marks left on
some wooden stumps where lumberjacks used to fasten their rafts.

The floating rafts were a unique scene of grandeur in Changbai Mountain.
The remarkable log-rafts would be lined up for several kilometers, fast floating
down the Yalu or Songhua river. The current in the Yalu River was swift. When
the rafts floated through rapids, they would bump into each other in waves,
appearing and disappearing now and then. On this risky journey, the lumberjacks had been trained to be quick-minded to deal with any unexpected situations.
Though very experienced, they still had to be extremely careful when passing
dangerous shoals, reefs or precipitous cliffs. To them, such places were like the
gates of hell.

Changbai Mountain under snow.

Log-rafts floating down the Yalu
River, a magnificent view.

Along the Yalu River, there were more than 80 dangerous points. Even extraordinarily brave and skilled lumberjacks could not avoid the possibility of injury or even death, so they placed their wagers on an invisible god, in hopes of a safe journey. So, a special rule of worshipping the river god was established in this trade, which has passed down to this day as a unique tradition. In the ceremony, the lumberjacks usually make offerings such as pig head and homemade wine, burn incense, and pray for safety.

After they had successfully brought the rafts to their destination, the lumberjacks would usually spend a lot of their hard-earned money to amuse themselves. To them, this work was not just for a living but also for the spiritual fulfillment in harnessing nature.

However, most of all, the lumberjacks longed for true love and happy family lives. They cared more about love and friendship than money. And in many a young woman's eyes, they were indeed true heroes.

Rafting on the Yalu River

In the 1990s, the Chinese government closed off numerous mountains, including Changbai Mountain, in order to facilitate regeneration of the forests. The amount of trees fell decreased drastically, resulting in a continuous reduction in the number of log-rafts on the Yalu. In 1995, Song Yan, the last lumberjack in Changbai County retired, marking the end of this age-old trade and the presence of the *muba* in the Changbai Mountain area.

Although the lumberjacks laboring strenuously on the Yalu River have disappeared, the tradition they brought into being has passed down. Rafting on the Yalu River has now turned into a new tourist draw.

Of all rafting routes in the world, that along the Yalu River may be the only cross-border one. This route starts from the ancient ferry in Changchuan, passes through Jangheung-ri in the Democratic People's Republic of Korean, the sandbank, ancient barracks, Xinchangdong, Shangchangli, and finally ends at Jinwozi of Changchuan. Along this approximately 12.5-km-long rafting route, the Yalu River is sometimes as smooth as a mirror, and sometimes becomes torrential. While drifting down the river, you will have the chance to experience so many different cultures as well as the natural scenery of different ethnic people. When the raft is rushing down along rapid currents, tourists easily get wet, with the coolness of the water immediately seeping through the entire body. At noon, when the sun shines on your back, it feels most warm and comforting. At night, you can stay in an old hut left by the lumberjacks — a must for tourists. These huts are actually ones from the past. When the rafts stop at a pier, tourists disembark to visit the old lumberjacks' temporary accommodations and the site where they used to assemble the rafts. Tourists can also set up a bonfire for wild game barbeque, to get a little bit of knowledge of lumberjacks' life with their own experience.

The raftsmen controlling the rafts for tourists are all lumberjacks in the old time, now retired. Not used to staying idle at home, they come back to take up their old trade. At the requests of tourists, they would often sing their old work songs. Their singing, together with the green mountains on the banks and swift currents down under, might bring your mind back to the old days.

Rafting on the Yalu River. ▶

Ginseng Traders in Northeast China

   In the mornings, the source of the Songhua River is permeated with a special kind of fragrance. This fragrance has, in fact, been smelt there for several centuries. But, in the cities those rushing to work every morning cannot smell it. Only when you visit Fusong, the largest ginseng market in China, would you be able to figure out the source of this lovely fragrance. Fusong, a town at the bottom of Changbai Mountain, has developed with the ginseng trade.

"The Hunt" for Ginseng

When the eighth lunar month comes every year, farmers living at the foot of Changbai Mountain will start to bake big pancakes. This type of food was brought there by people of earlier generations when braved their way to northeast China for a living. It is an ideal food for Ginseng hunters since it could be preserved for a month. The ginseng hunters set out on their long and dangerous journey with these big pancakes. Such a journey was usually called "a hunt."

Ginseng hunting was a seasonal job because only when the ginseng berry turned red could it be distinguished from other herbs. It is one of the oldest and most legendary means of sustenance for the old-time migrants to northeast China. Ginseng is a special produce of Changbai Mountain. Considered a "magical herb" or "immortal's medicine," it was said to be able to prolong one's life span and even bring the dead back to life. Ginseng had been a main source of wealth for the Qing Dynasty before it was established, worshipped by the Manchu ancestors as something with supernatural

power. It is said that Nurhachi (1559-1626, founder and first khan of Great Jin, or Later Jin, predecessor of the Qing Dynasty) was almost killed while hunting ginseng when he was young. Huangtaiji (1592-1643, second khan of Later Jin) made a shrine for a ginseng seedling in his bedroom. Later, Emperor Qianlong (1711-1799) wrote around 10 poems about ginseng.

In the early Qing Dynasty, smallpox had taken many people's lives. It was believed that only ginseng could cure this disease. Yet for a very long time, ginseng had been controlled by a single man — the emperor. It was impossible for common people to acquire it. At that time, the yearly output of ginseng was

lower than 5 kg. Only those officials who had accomplished meritorious deeds would be granted a little. Therefore, ginseng was priceless. Therefore, the mid-18th century witnessed a wave of ginseng hunting, when nearly 10,000 people set out in search of this magical plant.

It became a true contest. But, since it had to be done secretly back then, the ginseng hunters invented their own lingo. For example, they called ginseng, "wooden cudgels," and called digging ginseng, "hunting." In order to avoid being attacked by wild animals or becoming lost, ginseng hunters usually proceeded in groups of at least three. The main roles in each group were "the chief," "the rear" and "the cook." The chief would usually be most familiar with the forest and roads. Even if they became lost, the chief could easily guide everyone out. Thus, he was the person whom the group most relied on.

Ginseng grew wild in deep forests. As a short plant, it was difficult to distinguish. So, the hunters had to wield 1.5-m-long sticks to push the grass and leaves aside. In this way, they could check carefully, but had to move very slowly. Ginseng root is shaped like human body, thus its name. Its branches each carry five leaves, like an open palm of a hand. If a branch has six leaves, the ginseng root is considered to be of the highest quality, and possibly several hundred years old. This type of ginseng was the ginseng hunters' dream treasure.

On the mountains, many plants resemble ginseng, so the hunters were required to have sharp eyes. In order not to tire out their eyes, they needed to rest every couple of hours. Whenever they stopped, countless mosquitoes would plague them. Northeastern tobacco was employed as an ideal means to repel the mosquitoes. This way of repelling mosquitoes perhaps dates back to over 200 years ago, when ginseng hunters did not dare to light fires to drive away insects and wild animals, for if they were discovered by government patrols, they would have been exiled. Interestingly, after more htan 200 years later, ginseng hunting disappeared but the northeastern tobacco has been passed down.

There was no fixed route for hunting ginseng. Yet, it seemed that some invisible force guided the hunters. Ginseng was mostly found on steep mountain slopes or where there was a lot of Korean pine and toothed oak. It was rarely found elsewhere. But there were exceptions. For instance, the most valuable ginseng in history was said to have been found growing in a hole two m up a tall tree. The person who found it was extremely lucky.

However, the forests were filled
with too many uncertainties. Even once
they had located their dream ginseng,
this did not necessarily mean success.
The next step, of digging it out, was even
harder. The ginseng fiber could not be
broken. If any fibers were broken, the
value of the ginseng would drop.

▲ Dialogue between the spring and the winter.

▼ A natural scene on Changbai Mountain or a
Chinese ink and wash.

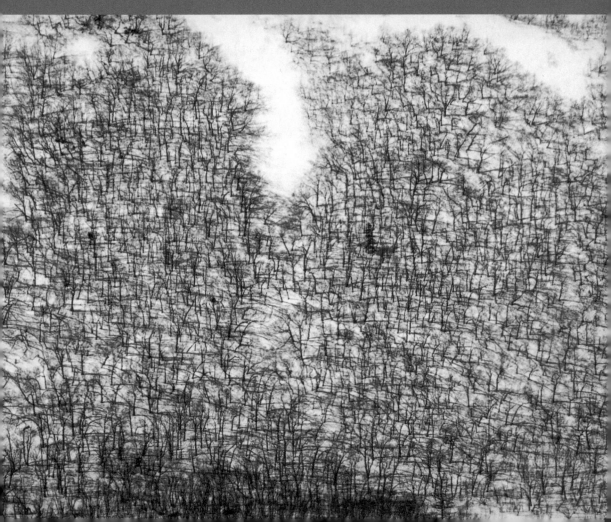

Mysterious Ginseng-digging Customs

It was said that ginseng was a naughty spirit always moving about. Some people might find a ginseng seedling, but when they dug it out, they discovered just an empty shell. Therefore, in order to prevent the ginseng from escaping, the ginseng hunters would use red string and coins to tie up the ginseng seedlings tightly, and then remove the dirt bit by bit around the seedling with a peg made of antler. Only after five or six hours of digging, might the ginseng's root finally fall into their hands. This human-shaped entity was the embodiment of the ginseng hunters' life dreams.

Ginseng hunters usually brought alcohol and meat with them from afar, to hold a grand ceremony at the site they managed to find the ginseng. Through the ceremony, they expressed their gratitude to a deified ginseng hunter named Sun Liang, a native of Laiyang, Shandong. It is said that Sun Liang and his sworn brother had braved a long difficult trek to Changbai Mountain in order to search for ginseng for their ailing mother. On the journey, the two became accidentally separated. Sun Liang looked for his brother for three days, without eating anything, ultimately starving to death. This man who

Ginseng produced in Jilin.

130

died for his brother was thus deified by ginseng hunters. People say he became a white-bearded old man who shows lost people the way out, and also guides them to where there is ginseng. His spirit supported many men who tried to make a living in northeast China. The 16th day of the third lunar month is Sun Liang's birthday. On this day, all ginseng collectors, lumberjacks and hunters would hold banquets to worship Sun Liang, as a way of praying for safety. Ginseng hunters also were required to build small symbolic shrines with three tiles to worship the mountain deity.

Ginseng hunters used to be extremely careful about what they said. It was taboo to utter any ominous words. They often used the verbs "take," "hold" or "carry," because these words were more respectful. For example, they would say "take a meal," instead of "eat a meal"; when resting, they said " hold onto a stack"; when wanting to smoke, they said "take fire"; "hold a pot" meant to cook; "carry ginseng" meant "dig ginseng." Indeed, when they said "carry the ginseng," it represented a kind of personi-fication of the ginseng.

Legends claim that ginseng has a life span of about 1,000 years. But experts, after conducting tests, have proven that it can live for up to 400 to 500 years. Dry ginseng can still sprout when placed in alcohol. In Fusong, there are four pieces of such ginseng. One, farmer Xu Chenghui's ginseng, has been soaked in high-percentage alcohol for over 30 years, and is still growing. Why does ginseng have such a strong life? This still remains a mystery. A famous collector, Xu Yannian developed an interesting point of view, after observing over 1,000 wild ginseng: ginseng lives among families, and even clans, that have together struggled against the harsh forces of nature, helping them to survive over hundreds of years.

These legends about those who made their living in northeast China hunting gin-seng are now of the vanishing past, but their adventurous and indomitable spirit will forever linger over this land of ginseng.

Songhua River
— Jilin's Mother River

A Most Wondrous River

Water has vast significance for Jilin Province, and even the name of the province is related to water. Jilin, or *Wula* in the Manchu language, means "Along the River," referring to a place by the Songhua (Sungari) River. The southern source of the Songhua River is Tianchi Lake (Heavenly Pool) on Changbai Mountain. On its way to the Heilong River, which finally flows into the Sea of Okhotsk, the river merges with over 920 tributaries. Along this mother river, there are sudden rapids and swirls, shimmering ripples and flitting shadows, stony banks and sandy beaches, islands and forests, wetlands and bays, as well as white clouds and whirlpools, forests and coalmines, and fields of soybean and sorghum.

Two Sources Far Apart

The Songhua is a river unique among all other rivers in the world, for it has two sources that are thousand kilometers apart from each other. As mentioned above, the southern source is Tianchi Lake on Changbai Mountain. Water rushing down from the Tianchi Lake forms the Erdaobai River, which is held as the main source of the Songhua. The northern source is the Nenjiang River, originating in Yilehuli Mountain of the Greater and Lesser Hinggan Mountains. "Nenjiang" means "dark green water" in Mongolian. The southern and northern sources of the Songhua River meet at Sanchahe (under the jurisdiction of Fuyu County, Jilin) on the border between Jilin and Heilongjiang provinces. When the Songhua initially pours into the Heilong River, a certain section of the river appears in two colors — green and yellow, hence its name "Huntong (Mixing) River."

The Songhua is a charming major river. People could hardly imagine let alone describe its vigor and immensity, a beauty beyond compare. Our ancestors once used the word "reverence" to describe their feelings towards the southern source of the Songhua River, namely, Tianchi Lake on Changbai Mountain and its waterfalls. Even today, the natural reserve there still leaves some riddles unsolved.

What also makes the Songhua unique is the evolution of its name. At first, the river was not so named. From the Eastern Jin Dynasty (317-420) to the Northern and Southern Dynasties (420-589), the upper reaches of the river were called "Sumo River," while the lower reaches were called "Nanshui River." During the Sui (581-618) and Tang (618-907) dynasties, the name for upper reaches remained unchanged except an alteration of the first charcter, while that of the lower reaches was changed into "Nashui River." When it came to the Liao Dynasty (907-1125), both upper and lower reaches

◀ Songhua River, the mother river for people of Jilin.

of the river came to be known as "Huntong River," or "Yazi (Duck) River." By the Jin Dynasty (1115-1234), the upper reaches were named "Songwa River," and the lower reaches "Huntong River." In the Yuan Dynasty (1271-1368), both the upper and lower reaches were known as "Songwa River." The name "Songhua River" was not used until the reign period of Xuande in the Ming Dynasty (1368-1644). Everyone knows there are pinecones and pine seeds, but no pine flowers. But, why the name "Songhua" (literally "pine flowers") was chosen as the name of the river? The lumbermen in Changbai Mountain recount the following legend.

In time immemorial, Changbai Mountain and the Greater Hinggan Mountains were connected, pine tree that grew in these mountains used to flower. At that time, many rivers and streams crisscrossed and flew into the sea, and numerous lakes and ponds dotted the land. Among these waters was a large lake called Lake

Lotus. No matter whether it was summer or winter, the lake brimmed with lotus. Under the lotus leaves, shoals of fishes and clams played with each other. Every clam's shell contained a luminous pearl. On starlit nights, high in the skies and below on the waters, auspicious rays shone over the entire lake, making the lake appear like a place full of treasure. However, everything changed when an evil dragon with white wings and white scales, known as the Little White Dragon flew into this place of treasure. Initially, the dragon simply remained quietly at the lake bottom. But later, it began to turn nasty, turning the lake topsy-turvy. Gradually, the lotus withered, the fish disappeared, and as the clams closed up their shells, pearls no longer illuminated the lake. The clear lake became a pond with a bad stench. Sometimes, when the Little White Dragon flapped its wings suddenly, the resultant floods swept over an area several hundred square miles.

The evil behavior of the Little White Dragon enraged the old Dragon King in the East Sea, who sent a dragon with black wings and black scales to subdue it. The black dragon fought three battles with Little White Dragon, but was defeated in the first two. The next summer, when the land was covered with white pine flowers, the surface of the rivers and lakes were also full of the flowers. The black dragon had an idea: he went to the Changbai Mountain and Greater Hinggan Mountains and shook down all the pine flowers to cover the water. Below the white pine flowers, the black dragon hid itself and ambushed the Little White Dragon in the Lake Lotus. Finally, he subdued the Little White Dragon after a fierce fight of three days and three nights. The black dragon later changed all the rivers and lakes into three major rivers, namely, Heilong, Wusuli and Songhua, as we now see. As the water ebbed, Lake Lotus eventually transformed into the crescent-shaped "Wu Da Lian Chi" (Five Big Lotus Ponds). The Greater Hinggan Mountains and Changbai Mountain were also broken up.

From then on, the pine no longer bloomed. To commemorate the services of the black dragon and the role played by the pine flowers, people called the river "Songhua."

◄ Source of the three rivers.

139

A Charming "Heavenly River"

In the language of the Manchus, the name for Songhua River is "Song'aliwula," meaning "Heavenly River." In remote antiquity, water from Tianchi Lake (Heavenly Pool) rushed down a thousand miles through high mountains and deep valleys, forests and the snow plains, and, in its vast bosom and with rich resources, nurtured the sons and daughters of various ethnic groups and gave birth to a simple and unconstrained culture.

▶ Soybean plants at the foot of Changbai Mountain.

The ancient people nurtured by Songhua River were called Northeastern *yi* (a name given to ancient tribes in the northeast) in ancient Chinese records. Of these *yi* tribes in the northeast, the Sushens, living north of Changbai Mountain around the southern source of the Songhua and in the Mudanjiang valley and on the lower reaches of the Songhua, were the first to establish close relations with the Chinese central plains. As early as 2,500 years ago, they came to the central plains to attend the massive assemblies of various tribes, bringing with them locally made bows and arrows as well as moose and reindeer as tribute. This relationship lasted for many long years. Thus, it was recorded in the *Spring and Autumn Annals*: "The Sushens live in the north of our land." The Donghus, who lived on the right bank of the Nenjiang River and the mountainous grasslands, gradually rose in power during the Han, Wei, Jin as well as Northern and Southern dynasties. Their offspring, including the Yuwen, Murong, and Tuoba tribes, built up their own local regimes. Along with them, there were also the Fuyu, Yilou, Wuji and Mohe tribes residing in the arm of the mother river. In addition, there were also the Yelü tribe (the royal family of the Liao Dynasty) of Qidan people originated from the land of pine forests; the Wanyan tribe (the royal family of the Jin Dynasty) living by the Haigu River (today's Haigou River) and the Anchuhu River (today's Ashi River); and the Mengwu Shiwei tribe who had once lived northeast of the upper Nenjiang River. Genghis Khan and Kublai Khan, two well-

◀ Crops produced in black soil.

▶ Corn belt in Jilin.

⏩ A view of the fertile black soil.

known figures in Chinese and world history, were descendants of the Mengwu Shiwei tribe. With the rise of the Nüzhen (today's Manchu), their leader Nurhachi established the Khanate of Later Jin after unifying all the tribes of the Nüzhens, and his progeny ultimately founded China's last mighty feudal empire — the Qing Dynasty. These people are all sons and daughters of the Songhua River, nourished on the nectar of the mother river.

The Songhua is a great creator. South of the river, it created the Songliao Plains, together with the Liaohe River; in the north, it created the alluvial Songnen Plains with its northern tributary Nenjiang River; and in its lower reaches, it brought into being the Sanjiang (Three-River) Plains, together with the Heilong and Wusuli rivers. These three plains of the Songhua produce thousands of miles of fertile soil. Abundant in soybean, corn, sorghum and wheat, they have wrought a huge granary of China, with high-quality flax, cotton, tobacco, apple and sugar beet as well.

The Songhua is a river of plenty. Mountains after mountains in the valley of the Songhua are covered with virgin forests. The lumber of the Greater and Lesser Hinggan and Changbai Mountain total one billion cubic meters. This is China's largest forest area. The areas watered by the Songhua also abound in mineral resources. Besides coal, there is also gold, copper, iron, etc. In the river, there are abundant carp, crucian carp, variegated carp (*Aristichthys nobli*), whitefish, *Hucho taimen Pallas*, *Nibea albiflora*, Amur ide (*Leuciscus waleckii*), etc., with an annual output totaling over 40 million kg. Especially, the Siberian great sturgeon (*Huso dauricus*), often 4 m to 5 m long and several tons in weight, is the largest fish found in all inland waters. During the Qing Dynasty, Siberian great sturgeon was presented as a tribute to the imperial family; common people were prohibited to eat it. People raised them in fishponds after catching them from the rivers, and they were sent to Beijing in carts when the rivers froze over.

The navigable length of the Songhua is 1,447 km. It is navigable upstream as far as Harbin, with steamships of 1,000 tons or more. Small river steamers use the Nenjiang River as far as Qiqihar, and the Songhua itself as far as Jilin City; while several of the other tributaries, like the Mudanjiang River and the Tongken River as well as the upper waters from Qiqihar to Nenjiang County on the Nenjiang, are navigable by small craft. The period when the waters are not frozen is from mid-April to early November.

In terms of the social and economic significance of the Songhua to agricultural and industrial production, inland shipping and people's lives in northeast China, it ranks much greater than other rivers in this area. Thus, the Songhua has been dubbed the "mother river" by the local people.

◄ Plain land in central Jilin.

Gentle and Harsh "Unsealing River"

From mid-November each year, ice appears at the lower reaches of the Songhua. Countless needles of ice crystals are formed in the river at low temperatures. The ice crystals accumulate gradually into ice floating with the river. Starting from the banks, water on the river surface is frozen into thin sheets of ice, slowly spreading to the center of the river. As the temperature lowers, the ice sheets begin to tightly fix the floating ice, forming an ice cap on the river. This process is called "sealing the river," meaning its freezing over. There are two types of "sealing," namely "gentle sealing" and "harsh sealing." Floating ice on the river is frozen into a relatively smooth cover as the temperature drops bit by bit, which is called "gentle sealing"; whereas "harsh sealing" is totally different. Large and small floating ice blocks collide with and crush each other in the cold wind. When the temperature suddenly drops, everything freezes together instantaneously. Therefore, on the icebound river surface, erect blocks of ice are seen scattered everywhere.

The frozen period of the Songhua is very long. The ice cap grows deeper with the cold winds. It is often nearly 40 cm thick by early December, 98 cm in January, and 140 cm at its maximum. The earlier beauty, of waves shimmering in the sunlight, disappears. Vehicles and walking people come and go directly on the frozen river surface, instead of ships and swimmers.

In mid-April the following year, sunshine, moderate breezes and drizzle bring spring back. The ice cap on the river gradually thaws into big and small pieces of ice flowing with the river, known as "unsealing the river." There are also two types of

"unsealing": "gentle unsealing" and "harsh unsealing." On bright and balmy days, the river thaws slowly, being the "gentle unsealing." Adversely, on windy days, the water flows much more quickly, hence pressing heavily on the ice. As a result, the ice breaks. Huge ice blocks are lifted up high, and drop suddenly in the billows of the river, referred to as "harsh unsealing."

Scenes of rushing ice floes, as the river thaws, are truly magnificent. When the temperature rises gradually, the ice cap thaws into countless sheets of ice of different size. One by one, they go downstream with the river, mildly and quietly, like moving sheep flocks and white clouds. The floating ice floes crumple on the banks, making small sounds. This is the scene of the "gentle unsealing" of the river. The scene of ice floes rushing in "harsh unsealing" presents quite a different picture: Sudden rises in temperature or sudden warm breezes thaw the steel-hard ice cap in an instant, cracking. With ice blocks as large as a house or as small as cobblestones, they rush down; the ice floes bump, crash and jumble into each other in the process. With the force of a landslide, and the power of a tidal wave, like charging troops of thousands, the process is absolutely irresistible.

Every year, when the ice cap thaws into running ice floes, local people always go down to the riverbank to watch the scene, as a special outing. The vanishing of the ice floes means the warm spring is on its way back. After being frozen over for six months, the Songhua recovers its vibrancy and life. The river begins to flow smoothly, as water birds hover over it happily.

The Last Fishing and
Hunting Tribe

In satellite photographs, one can easily locate China's two famous water systems — the Songhua and the Nenjiang — from the south and north respectively, converging in western Jilin Province. West of the point of convergence lies China's seventh largest fresh water lake — Qagan Nur, which is 420 sq. km in size. Two rivers and a lake meet here, looking like a deity folding together his palms to hold a shining pearl on the Nen Horqin Grasslands. This area is Qian Gorlos Mongol Autonomous County, where the world's oldest fishing and hunting tribe still lives.

Fishers on Qagan Nur

"Gorlos" is from the Mongolian language, where "Gor" means "river" and "Los" is "water." Therefore, "Gorlos" means "river water." In Mongolian, "Qian Gorlos" is the same as "South Gorlos," as the ancient Chinese always referred to directions according to the flow of the river. In this case, the word "qian" actually meant the south bank of the Nenjiang River. Because of this, people usually call the flat land here "Nenjiang Plains." As this area was once the eastern part of the Horqin Grasslands, it also acquired the name "Nen Horqin."

Qagan Nur is located in the northwest of Mongolian Autonomous County of Qian Gorlos. With a capacity of some 700 million cubic meters of water, it is 2.5 m deep on average. The zigzagging lakeshore reaches 128 km. It is a famous aquatic production center and an important wetland nature reserve of Jilin Province, teeming with 68 fish varieties of 15 families, including carp, chub, variegated and crucian carp, as well as shrimp, reeds and pearls. A legend tells of a time when Gorlos had just formed its shape like a Mongolian boot, an old man once lived here. Carrying a *matou qin* (traditional Mongolian bowstring instrument) on his back, he was herding his only white cattle and white sheep. One day, he suddenly saw a hundred swans flying from the horizon to hover in the sky a hundred times, and then return to the north. Gusts of wind immediately blew in the direction the swans had departed, followed by a downpour. A divine horse with two wings appeared in the sky, and landed in a place faraway.

▶ A ferry in winter.

At that moment, the downpour ceased and rainwater formed a lake. The old herder went to the shore, and looked at the mirror-like clear lake that resembled a full moon. Hence, he called the lake "Qagan Nur," a name that has been passed down generation after generation. In the Mongolian language, "Qagan" means "moon."

As last remnants of the fishing and hunting culture in the world, everything in the villages by Qagan Nur, is closely related to "fishing." Fishing nets are aired in the yards, on the roofs and walls; the smell of fish wafts through the air; and fish is even the theme on children's schoolbag designs, women's paper-cuts for window decoration and couplets in all households. People here have organized themselves as the world's last ancient fishing and hunting tribe. For thousands of years, they moved from place to place in search of water and grass, believing that water is sacred, as the source of "good." Fishing in winter on Qagan Nur over the long history has gained fame both at home and abroad. Therefore, people even called people living here "Qagan Nur fisherfolk," though they are actually herders. ·

In this area, the fishermen are called *yuba* (fishing gang). Here, the character *ba* means "gang." The head of a fishing gang must have extraordinary skills, and he is the leader and mainstay of the

fishermen. According to *Records of Investigation into Gorlos*, there was once a famous fishing gang leader named Sun in one of the villages. With his acute eyes, he could find shoals of fish below the deep ice cap, and with his ears he could hear the sound of fish under the ice. All these skills actually came from his knowledge and experience gained through living by Qagan Nur.

Ice and snow cover all of Qagan Nur in the winter. The ice reaches one to two meters in depth. Yet, winter is the best season for the local fishermen to catch fish. The methods they employed to catch fish under ice are numerous, using either fishing nets or fishing hooks. The fish net used is several hundred meters long. To insert it through the ice cap needs skill. Before casting a net, the key approach is to select the right place. Experienced fishers can determine when and where to cast the nets just by surveying the color of the ice. Having decided where to cast the nets, they will drill two rows of holes through the ice and insert the head-rope into water under ice, then gradually close the net and draw in it through a large hole drilled beforehand for the purpose. In the winter, fish crowd together under the ice. So, with a large net, one catch is able to bring in thousand kilograms of fish.

▼ Winter fishing on Qagan Nur.

Offering Sacrifices to the Lake for Fishing

Now, the winter fishing season at Qagan Nur lasts from mid-December to mid-January of the following year. The total annual output may reach one million kilograms. In the biting cold, thousands of people work on the ice; dozens of trucks transport day upon night, and thousands of kilograms of fresh fish are caught in the water every day, a dazzling scene rarely seen throughout China and even the world.

The fishing and hunting culture of Qagan Nur has a long history. It began in prehistoric times, and has prospered since the Liao and Jin dynasties. Attracted by lush water grass, crowded geese and ducks, emperors of the Liao Dynasty, from Emperor Shengzong to Emperor Tianzuo, came here each year for the spring hunt and winter fishing by cutting holes in the ice cap. They held the ceremonial "first fish banquet" and "first goose banquet." Since it is easier to preserve, transport and process fish in winter, winter thus turns out to be the golden season for catching and eating fish in the northern land. The millennium-old tradition of winter fishing on Qagan Nur lasts to this day. In the heyday of the kingdom established by the Qidans in northeast China, the kings used to call in ministers to the ice cap of the Songhua River to enjoy themselves with fishing. Their tradition of entertaining guests was even more interesting. When a distinguished guest came from afar to visit the Qidan kingdom in winter, the hosts would pitch a tent on the ice cap of the river, and then rub iron against the ice until the ice was thin enough and transparent. The hosts and guests would amuse themselves together by watching the fish swimming under the ice. At banquet time, the host would smash a hole on the ice to let fish jump out the hole. They would catch it on the spot and have it prepared to serve.

A sacrifice-offering ceremony is always conducted before winter fishing on Qagan Nur. The Nen Horqin Grasslands give those hunting and fishing and living there over a long history, a suntanned complexion, strong build and chiseled firm features. Honoring the heaven as the father and the earth as the mother, they make offerings during the ceremony in hope that all beings will prosper forever and their catches would be plenty.

A hole about one meter in diameter is dug in the ice for throwing in the offering. A red table is set in front of it, and placed on it are stir-fried millet, butter and cheese, as well as burning incense. When the beginning of the ceremony is announced, lamas start turning their wheels of Dharma, Mongolian youth in colorful clothes and fierce masks start performing the Qama Dance, the heads of the fishing gangs followed the procession of lamas and danc-

ing youth to the opening in the ice, while fishermen stand in a row by horse-drawn sleds loaded with fishnets. In this moment, the sutra chanting, the rich scent of burning sandalwood incense, and the extraordinary costumes in bright colors, all constitute a beautiful painting of folk customs. After circling the hole three times, the heads of the fishing gangs throw all the offerings into the opening, and then lead the fishermen to jump onto their sleds and rush far out onto the lake, in the midst of sutra chanting and singing. Thus, the winter fishing begins.

In recent years, "red nets" (implying good harvest of fish) have frequently appeared in winter fishing on Qagan Nur. The biggest single catch in 2005 reached 50,000 kg, while the biggest fish that was caught was a 20-kg bighead. The bigheads living in the totally unpolluted environment of Qagan Nur are large and fleshy. Since the fish is quite tender and delicious, it is the most precious dish in the fish banquets of Qagan Nur. It is also listed as a kind of environmentally "green" food by the China Green Food Center.

Since 2003, the Mongolian Autonomous County of Qian Gorlos has held the "China Jilin Qagan Nur Winter Fishing Tourism Festival" every year. Many tourists have been attracted by the charms of this ancient fishing and hunting tribe in northern China.

Qian'an Earthen Forest:

Located on the east banks of Dabusu Lake in Qian'an County, Songyuan City, the Qian'an Earthen Forest, also known as "Wolf-teeth Flatland" to the local people for its wolf-teeth like shape, was formed by continuous erosion by rainwater of the seriously salinized lakeshore. The "Wolf-teeth Flatland" is 50 m higher than the water surface of Dabusu Lake and stretches 15 km north to south, covering an area of 58 sq. km. Although absent with towering peaks, it has steep cliffs everywhere. There are many creeks flowing across the earthen peaks. On the slope land, the vegetation is intact, forming a beautiful natural landscape. Fossils of 13 species of vertebrates have been excavated there, proving that, tens of thousands of years ago, large numbers of mammoths and other animals had lived in this area. Moreover, the stoneware, pottery ware, bronze ware and early coins relics discovered in the locality indicate that humans were active in the area from the time of the Neolithic Age thousands of years ago.

Homeland of Red-crowned Cranes

Nenjiang River, the northern source of the Songhua, flows through the Yilehuli Mountain of the Greater Hinggan Mountains. To the west of the Greater Hinggan Mountains is the Inner Mongolia Plateau, which tips down in the east to the Songnen Plains. There are dozens of rivers zigzagging eastward. The Hulin River, a branch of the Nenjiang River, is one of them. The river flows across the Horqin Grasslands and passes a place called Gaoliban into a wash at Tongyu County in western Jilin, at which the course of the river often becomes invisible. On the map, this section of the Hulin River becomes a dotted line, meaning that, at most times, the river course is dry. When the river ends in Tongyu County, it resembles a cracked mirror, that is, turning into numerous large and small shards, representing lakes, ponds, marshes and pools that are scattered over an 110,000-hectare area. Many traces here give evidence that this area was once a large water system.

This wash is called Xianghai Lake, a small lake between the Horqin Grasslands and the Songnen Plains.

"Xianghai" is literally "Sea of Xiang." Why would a small lake be called a "sea"? This is a natural question that comes to the mind of people who have never been to Xianghai. "Changbai in the east and Xianghai in the west," people in Jilin always describe the province's unique landscape with such a phrase. All people know here "Changbai" refers to the Changbai Mountain. But, fewer people know Xianghai. Yet, when they are told that Xianghai is the homeland of red-crowned cranes, they will surely be amazed.

Xianghai is a national-level nature reserve, an important wetland of the world, and "a Class-A nature reserve of international importance," as rated by the World Wildlife Fund. Despite all these titles for the lake, people prefer to call it "Xianghai Wetlands." In the eyes of the local people, the lake is a treasure fallen from the heavens, for it is not only the home of the "Immortal Crane" (pet name for the red-crowned crane), but also of the wild Mongolian elm (*Ulmus propinqua*), a "living fossil" no larger than an arm despite growing for a hundred years.

Into the Nature Reserve

Xianghai lies quietly in the arms of the Horqin Grasslands. The gentle Hulin River flows slowly through the land, telling stories of the crane's homeland with every drop of water. Xianghai is an integral part of the Horqin Grasslands. Long ago, the grassland was as famous as Xilin Gol and Hulun Buir. In history, the Horqin Grasslands, including Xianghai, were the abode of one tribe under Genghis Khan, producing Genghis Khan's unbeatable cavalries that once swept over the Asia and Europe.

Upon entering the Xianghai Nature Reserve, what comes to people's vision first is the boundless Xianghai Lake. The smaller lakes and marshes are connected with the quietly flowing river. On the undulating dunes stand Mongolian elms in different forms and postures like pot culture. Various kinds of birds fly over the marshes, filling the air with their song. In the ponds scattered all through the marsh, cattails and reeds grow thickly. Crane, egret and other waterfowl fly or swim over water, singing and dancing. Cattle and sheep cover the vast grasslands. Roe deer, rabbit, corsac fox and badger frequently appear and disappear. And fish swim in the clear waters. Along with the fishermen, shepherds, cooking smoke and farmhouses, the scene makes for a natural painting, a fresh and chaste pastoral poem.

In Xianghai, every life has the right and space to live and grow. The Xianghai Nature Reserve boasts nearly 600 species of wildlife, among which 220 are medicinal plants and 300 birds, of which 52 birds in severe danger of extinction are under the national level I and II protection. In the Changlong Rare Waterfowl Observation Station, people can pinpoint through telescopes various birds from water to sky, from marsh to grass. There are many rare species. The six species of crane living here, accounting for 40 percent of the world's total, tell us how good the environmental quality is. Well over 30 animals, such as Mongolian gazelle,

▲ Xianghai Nature Reserve.

rabbit, wolf, fox, weasel and fitch, live in the jungles and on the grassland. In August, when you place your foot on the grass, dozens of grasshoppers jump out. They are the favorite food of birds.

Very long ago, nomadic peoples moved here to herd their cattle and sheep. Some of them settled down — the ancestors of today's Xianghai people. A nation on horseback, they also learned to stand on boats. Generation after generation, year after year, time passed with the sounds of the oar and scull. At present, people in Xianghai still maintain their traditions and customs. Except for a few occupied with tourism, most still lead a fishing or herding life, going to work at dawn and returning home at sunset. To protect the ecological system, they use ducks and other birds to catch and eat pests, such as grasshoppers, instead of using pesticide. This not only increases the farmers' incomes, but also multiplies the numbers of birds, such as geese, crane and ibis. More and more migrating birds fly to the south of China every year, benefiting the southern areas too.

Prince Bernhard of the Netherlands called Xianghai, "a wonderland on the earth." George Archibald, president of the International Crane Foundation, also showered praises on the region, saying that places like Xianghai, with its superb natural scenery, primeval ecological systems and diverse wetland creatures, are rare in the world, although he had visited many nature reserves in over 50 countries. Xianghai is truly a land of treasure in China, and in the world.

This is Xianghai, a small "sea." During the dry and hot days of northern China, it brings people some coolness and wetness; and through the wilderness of the Horqin Grasslands, it brings people a patch of green. It is a place for travelers to rest, a place for migrating birds to lay eggs, and a place for a varied range of animals to inhabit. Xianghai has a certain powerful lure compelling people to return to nature, and purifying their souls.

◄ Wetland in the Xianghai Nature Reserve.

Dancing with Red-crowned Cranes

Nature brings numerous birds to Xianghai. The monsoon climate creates such a clear seasonal ecological transition, telling the birds when to fly south, and when to return.

The total area of the Xianghai Nature Reserve is 105,000 ha, of which 36,000 ha are wetland. The vast reed marshes, flourishing with float grass, is the best place for the birds to build nests and rear their young. Of the world's remaining 1,500 red-crowned cranes that inhabit northeast China, Xianghai has more than 100.

The red-crowned cranes have unadorned white feathers, elegant and well-groomed figures, as well as a clear and melodious singing. In ancient Chinese myths and legends, they were called "immortal cranes," symbolizing elegance, longevity, wisdom and diligence. *The Book of Songs*, China's earliest collection of poetry, includes a poem titled "Singing Crane." Before bird experts discovered the significance of the red-crowned cranes' singing, their beautiful voices had long echoed over Xianghai. The red-crowned crane has brought to Xianghai a certain dynamism. They have their own childhood, their own romantic love, and their own family love and happiness. They dwell in the wetland's grasslands and reed marshes. Every spring and autumn, they become quite active here, singing and dancing. When they play and sing in couples, their sounds can echo several kilometers away, expressing their faith in love. The red-crowned crane is a very clever and beautiful bird. They have strong family bonds, and only take one lifelong partner. At one time, a number of wild cranes flew to Xianghai and mated with domesticated cranes. From then on, the wild cranes have kept flying back to the reserve in spring for union with their mates, although they still fly south when winter approaches.

◄ Red-crowned cranes, bird of Jilin, in the Xianghai Nature Reserve.

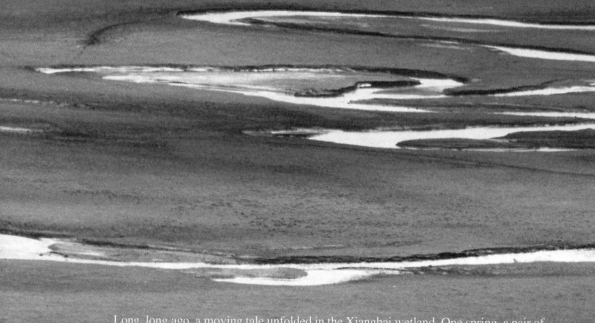

Long, long ago, a moving tale unfolded in the Xianghai wetland. One spring, a pair of cranes flew back to Xianghai from afar. They had no time to rest before building their nest, as the female crane was about to lay eggs. However, in the summer of that very year, severe floods spread, sweeping away many birds' nests and eggs. Their nest and eggs were no exception. After the flood, the crane couple rebuilt their nest, the female crane laid her eggs again, and gave birth to a baby crane. Unfortunately, by the time the little crane began learning to fly awkwardly, winter was already approaching. With piercing cold invading the air, the other cranes had already flown south. The crane duo taught the little crane to fly day and night. They sensed the danger when the first snow was falling. They sang to the little crane, urging it to grasp the skills of long-distance flight as quickly as possible, otherwise their family would freeze to death in the snow. The little crane understood its parents, but its thin feathers and weak physical strength could not bear up to any long-distance flying. Not much later, winter came with snow and ice. The crane family disappeared in the cold wind and snow. Local residents no longer heard the singing of the little crane while it was learning to fly in the snow. But that little crane, killed by the winter, never felt alone, for its parents held it close under their wings even as they were dying, trying to bestow their last warmth on the little one. When spring returned, familiar pleasant sounds also returned from the sky. Cranes back from the south happily sang, as if saying, "Home is Xianghai." The elders of Xianghai always tell children this moving story, teaching them to honor and love nature, because they themselves are a part of nature.

The moving documentary *Home Is Xianghai* won three international awards in 1991.

The beautiful Xianghai Nature Reserve, with its plentiful eco-resources, is an appeal to all bird experts and bird lovers.

The red-crowned crane is the spirit of Xianghai. Xianhe (Immortal Crane) Isle, surrounded by water on three sides and by hills on the fourth, has lush shrubbery and reeds and countless birds. In the Rare Birds Zoo are gathered together the majestic oriental white crane, the sharp-witted gray crane, the exquisite and cute demoiselle crane, and the elegant red-crowned crane. The red-crowned cranes partly reared in the wilds are, no doubt, the most important "stars" of the isle. These tall birds, with their coat of white feathers and black plumes, are elegant, pretty and neat. Apart from their red crown and dark yellowish green beaks, they have almond eyes and a brown iris, like fairies from traditional Chinese paintings. Red-crowned cranes like people. They sometimes walk in the grass along the lake like ladies, sometimes dance like white fairies, and sometimes play with the tourists, eating corn off their palms. When the zoo lets the cranes fly outside, with several peals of song, a dozen or more cranes spread out their wings and fly up to the sky. They flit among the tourists and bring their "catch" up to the sky. The red-crowned cranes, like natural angels, fly graciously between the sky and the earth, linking nature and humans closer together.

Grassland in west Jilin.

Poultry farm in Xianghai's wetlands.

Sacred Elms in "Sea of Incense"

Xianghai was once called Xianghai (Sea of Incense or 香海 in Chinese) Temple, and to this day even some maps are still marked with this name. Around the fifth century, Tibetan Buddhism began to become popular on the grasslands. Since the vegetation in Xianghai was luxuriant and the landscape was beautiful, a large number of lamas came here from afar to spread Tibetan Buddhism. Not far away from Xianghai Lake lies the 3,000-sq.m Xianghai Temple ruins. At that time, the area was property of a Mongolian king. When Lamaism arose on the grasslands, the king invested in a magnificent Lamaist temple at the site. It was said that the 13th Dalai Lama once preached in the temple, for which the temple gained even greater fame. Because so many people went to the temple to burn incense and pray, the incense smoke floating up to the sky amassed like a cloud. People called it the "Sea of Incense." Legend has it that, when Genghis Khan passed here, he saw this "white cloud" drifting from the distance. Amazed, he sent a guard to find out what it was. The guard returned and reported that there were thousands of lamas chanting Buddhist scriptures, and the clouds in the sky were from the burning incense. Genghis Khan nodded and remarked, "This is indeed a land of treasure." However, as time passed, the temple was gradually abandoned. Lamas left and the incense clouds disappeared. The temple fell

into shambles, with only some ruins remaining. Later, people forgot its original name, but miscalled it "Xianghai" (向海) ever since.

Close to the ruins of the Xianghai Temple stand five 800-year-old elms, guarding the temple like warriors. Strangely enough, the trees are coiled into forms of Chinese dragons. It is said that once Kublai Khan, or Emperor Shizu of Yuan Dynasty, went to the temple to worship the Buddha with his eight treasured horses. He ordered the chargers to be hitched to the elm trees in front of the temple. While he was offering incense to the Buddha, the sky suddenly split open with lightning and thunder, and a high wind sprang up. The horses became frightened. They reared and tried to run, pulling the elms so hard that they become coiled, finally breaking loose from their halters and galloping back to the Mongolian grasslands. Kublai Khan, sad about losing his horses, remained dazed in Xianghai for three days. Later, a Ming poet came to Xianghai and, seeing these five elms, wrote a poem praising the elms' firmness and strength. The poem runs like this:

Five elms stand proudly beside the great lake, uncaring of wind and rain.
Though the eight chargers have the power to move mountains,
They were shamed they could not hurt a tree root.

A view of the grassland.

Grazing on the grassland.

The coiling reveals their true spirit, and lowered heads a symbol of their firm will.
The horses breaking loose from halters galloped home,
Leaving Emperor Shizu to only weep.

Due to its saline-sodic soil, few crops and grass grow around Xianghai. Therefore, the area is not fit for farming or pasturing. However, on the meandering dunes of Xianghai grow elms of different shapes, covering two thirds of the land. The rarest is the Mongolian elm (*Ulmus propinqua*). It has an interesting crown resembling a mushroom umbrella. Xianghai's Mongolian elms are famous for their size, their old growth rings and their lovely poses. In Xianghai, certain Mongolian elms that are only three to four meters high may have survived for several 100 or even 1,000 years. Even trees one meter high are already 100 years old.

Mongolian elm is considered a sacred tree by the local people. It is said that the Mongolian elm was once a dragon-head-topped walking stick of the Immortal of the South Pole. One day, with this gold walking stick, the immortal was riding on a red-crowned crane to the three immortal's islands of Penglai, Fangzhang and Yingzhou to visit his Taoist friends. On his way passing Xianghai, he stopped to take in the scenery. He saw how mighty and vast the green waters and reed marshes were on the boundless grassland. On the lakes and rivers scattered over the land, birds sang and frolicked. Just as he was feeling the height of joy over all of these sights, a sudden wind blew up the sand, breaking up this poetic beauty. The god thought for a while, then threw his stick down at a cloud. Soon, stretches of Mongolian elm forests sprung up on the sand dunes of Xianghai, and the sandstorm stopped.

The Mongolian elm's coiling trunk is no thicker than a bowl's mouth. Trees in clumps all have their own unique shapes and gestures, with luxuriant foliage and spreading branches. Some trunks are tightened into a clinch; others lean on one another; while some intertwine together. In winter, when snow falls and the earth freezes over, the Mongolian elms stand out of the snow like small white mushrooms, resembling soft and delicious wild herbs. In summer, when the scorching sun shines over the earth and the heat becomes unbearable, the trees turn into sunshades on the dunes, providing a place for birds to build their nests, and multiply their families, and providing travelers with shade to rest under. When the rain passes and the sky clears, with the breeze,

the raindrops fall down along the leaves like glittering pearls. Seeing this, people may recall these lines: "A night of rain amongst the mountains, brings hundreds of springs on the treetops."

In the Mongolian elm forests, birds sing everywhere. On the treetops, in the shrubbery and among the grass under the trees, birds sing incessantly. There are also many raptors and beasts appearing in the woods. Walking through the deep forests, people may startle a vulture or a roe. If lucky enough, people may see a rare golden eagle open its bright eyes to stare at the uninvited guests. On the grassland, under the trees, moles are easy to find, working at their molehills. The numerous molehills, one in every half a meter, are the same in scale, shape and color. If people stamp their feet on the ground, moles at once will poke their necks out of the small hills (their burrow door), looking right into people's eyes. If they feel safe, they extend their claws to comb the long hair at their jaws, preening as if there were no one else around at all. If people pretend to catch them, they immediately draw back into the holes, and in a moment can be spotted poking out their heads from other molehills. It is truly a funny sight.

▲ Mongolian wrestlers.

▼ Wetland in Xianghai.

Jilin, a Riverside City

The city of Jilin is the pearl of the Songhua. It came into existence because of the river, stretched along the river, developed with the river, and has been beautified by the river.

Jilin was originally called "Jilin Ula." This was a Manchu name, meaning "city along the river." During the Ming-Qing period, for defense against foreign aggression, the government set up a shipyard here, which gave rise to its other name, "Chuanchang." ("shipyard" in Chinese). In 1674, Emperor Kangxi of the Qing Dynasty made an inspection tour of the naval base here. He penned the poem "Song of Ships on the Songhua," in which there is a line, "Numerous warships seek harbor in the riverside city." Since then, Jilin was also called "riverside city of northern China."

Jilin lies at the place where Changbai Mountain slopes to the Songliao Plains, and the Songhua River crosses the city in an "S" shape. The city is surrounded on all sides by Longtan Mountain, Xiaobai Mountain, Zhuque Mountain and Xuantian Mountain, which guard the city like the so-called celestial animals in Taoism, namely, the blue dragon, white tiger, red bird and black tortoise. In addition, there are Xituan Mountain and Dongtuan Mountain, both of which have in them ruins of ancient culture. The meandering river and the surrounding mountains bestow to the city a rather lovely landscape.

Jilin is China's only city with the same name as a province. It has also been listed by the State Council as a historic and cultural city. Jilin has the largest Confucian Temple in northeast China — the Jilin Confucian Temple built in 1742, in addition to the group of ancient Buddhist, Taoist and Confucian temples in mountains to the north, the Ashiha Dharma Cliff Inscriptions carved during the Ming Dynasty, the world's largest meteorolite, as well as various unique ethnic cultural traditions.

Jilin Rime, the Fourth Natural Wonder in China

The depths of winter in northern China offer desolate scenery of frozen lands. However, on the banks of the Songhua can still be found a wonderful scene — the Jilin rime, which is renowned as one of China's four natural wonders, along with the landscape of Guilin, the stone forest of Yunnan and the Three Gorges on the Yangtze River.

The snow-covered weeping willows and other trees along the banks of the Songhua in Jilin City seem to be made of jade, gleaming in the sunshine. Walking through the woods, people feel as if they were in a fairyland. Since 1991, Jilin city has held its annual "Ice and Snow Festival for Viewing Rime."

Rime, or frost coating, has two categories: grainy and crystal. The tightly structured grainy rime comes in tiny ice pellets, while crystal rime is relatively uncompressed, appearing like larger pieces of ice. The Jilin rime is of the crystal type, formed naturally in the special local geographical environment. Along the Songhua, about 15 km above Jilin City, is the Fengman Hydropower Station, where the water temperature remains above 4°C (39.2°F) even in the coldest winter, since the water warms up when flowing through the hydropower generators. Because of this, though the water flows quite slowly for dozens of kilometers through the city, it does not freeze. Instead, it provides sufficient vapor that in turn forms a fog that does not disperse. Moreover, there are many willows and pines on the banks. Under these conditions of a certain air pressure, temperature and wind direction, the fog on the river eventually freezes into rime over the trees. Jilin rime appears about 60 to 70 times each year in the last 10 days of November, up to March or April of the following year.

There are different things to watch at different times of the day, as the saying goes, "View fog at night; watch ice hangings in the morning; and enjoy falling 'flowers' at noon." "View fog at night" means to watch the foggy scene over the river in the early hours of the night before the rime is formed. At about 10 pm, a thin fog appears over the river, and then it expands and thickens. A great amount of white fog rises from the river, and moves to the riversides. "Watch ice hangings in the morning" means to watch the ice hanging down from the tree branches that have turned silver overnight. In early morning, the willows weep with jade teardrops, and clusters of pine needles resemble blossoming silver chrysanthemum, glittering and translucent. "Enjoy falling 'flowers' at noon" means to watch the falling ice pendants. Usually, at around 10 am, the ice hangings begin to fall, first one by one and then in larger numbers. When there is a breeze, the falling ice flies about and

▶ Jilin rime.

dances in the air, appearing like a colorful snow curtain in bright sunshine.

Aside from its beauty, rime is good for people's health. As people enjoy this beautiful creation of Nature, they may also feel the especially fresh air, comfortable for breathing. This is because rime on the trees has a property of purifying the air, in which large amounts of invisible dust float, threatening people's health. When rime begins to be formed, the vapor freezes and absorbs large amounts of dust particles. This works as an air "purifier" over large areas. Jilin rime is also a natural negative-oxygen-ion generator. Negative oxygen ions are called "vitamins," "environmental protectors," and "longevity elements" in the air. They can ease the mind, improve people's immunity and build up their health. Tests conducted reveal that there are a thousand or even several thousands of negative oxygen ions in every cubic centimeter of air along the banks of the Songhua in Jilin City when rime appears, five times more than when there is no rime. Moreover, Jilin rime is also a natural "silencer." As the Jilin rime is thick but loose, with many spaces in it, its reflectivity of sound is quite low. Since the rime absorbs sound waves, surrounded by it people feel as quiet as in a forest.

Jilin rime is well known, yet most people just view the rime at the 5-km stretch of riverbank in the city center. Only a few people know that the best place to enjoy the rime is the Rime Isle on the river. On the isle, rime appears almost every day during the winter, and sometimes the rime stays on the trees for several days.

The rime on the isle is exceptionally beautiful, thus giving rise to the name of the isle. The small island lies in a bay of the Songhua, 40 km north to the city. In mid-winter, the warm stream from the city passes around the isle, forming a lot of fog on the river. When the river wind blows, the fog turns into frost on the isle, coating trees and other plants, the fields and the farmhouses. Putong Village on the isle is the most ideal place for enjoying the rime.

That saying of "viewing fog at night, watching ice hangings in the morning, and enjoying falling 'flowers' at noon" holds a special meaning on this small island. On the isle, around 10 pm, a thin fog rises slowly from the river, looking more like cloud and smoke. Fog covers the land in the wild, enveloping all the people in an atmosphere of mysterious charm. In the morning, the isle is surrounded by mist. Looking out from the isle, forests on the other side of the river are hidden in mist, appearing to be gleaming. Over the quiet river, with white clouds rising, all things are only dimly discernible. The curves of remote mountains are shaped like fine eyebrows of girls. Forests are rimed and bamboo groves are frost-covered. All things seem as if found only in a dreamland. Then

► Fun with rime.

at noon, the glittering and translucent jade trees and branches make people feel as if they were inside a glazed palace.

It is a pity that the full poetic scene appears only rarely. Some people have been to the isle several times in hope of appreciating its most beautiful scenery, but without fulfilling their wish. Perhaps, the fleetingness of such a wonderful view only makes the Rime Isle more alluring, its rare beauty making the heart tremble even more.

On the isle, tourists may also enjoy themselves with true northeast China traditional recreational activities, such as northeast China *yangge* (yangko) dance, *er'renzhuan* (similar to song-and-dance duet), *zhua galaha* (toss-and-catch game popular in northeast China). The farmers of Hantun Village on the isle still live in Manchu-style *sanheyuan* (courtyard with houses built on three sides) and *siheyuan* (quadrangles). In the houses, traditions unique to the Manchus are evident, such as hearth walls, 万-shaped brick beds (heated and running along three inside walls) and wood-framed windows covered with paper. In the biting cold of winter, would there be anything more comforting than sitting on a heated brick bed, watching the silver white rime, tasting the famed Manchu dishes of "Stewed White Pork and Blood Sausage" and "Stewed Starch Noodles with Pork," while drinking big bowls of liquor and eating hearty chunks of meat?

◄ Rime on the banks of the river.

185

Three Types of Lanterns of Jilin

From time immemorial, every place around China has followed the tradition of watching colorful lanterns during the Lantern Festival (15th day of the first lunar month). However, watching three types of lanterns, namely, color lanterns, ice lanterns and river lanterns at the same time, was perhaps only possible in Jilin City. On the day of the festival, after eating dumplings with sweet stuffing (specially prepared for the occasion), all people in the city would go out of their houses and along the snowy streets to enjoy the lanterns. The color lanterns are gorgeous, while the enigmatic ice lanterns are mystifying, and the river lanterns flicker along the river like Chinese dragons. This splendid scene, with all the three types of lanterns reflecting each other, attracts all eyes.

The color lanterns, also known as "flower lanterns," of Jilin, have a long history. They originated in the imperial court. Particularly since 1991, when Jilin held the first "China (Jilin) Ice and Snow Festival for Viewing Rime," the scale of the lantern gatherings have continuously grown in size, while the activities grown in variety. Electronic automation, light effects and remote-control technology combine with the traditional lantern craft to create an innovative variety of lantern shapes and styles. Every year, great numbers of lanterns are exhibited, with over 4,000 at the height. During the festival, at nightfall the numerous lanterns light up the 5-km river bank, resembling the Milky Way in the sky. It is a scene of unspeakable wonders when the colorful lanterns' inverted reflections in the water glitter along with the lanterns flickering in the wind on the bank.

◄ Jilin — a wonderful riverside city.

► Ice lanterns in Jilin City.

Jilin City is the cradle of 300-year-old ice lanterns. Formerly, the ice lanterns were made by fishermen for the purpose of fishing during winter nights. In the old times, it was quite simple to make an ice lantern: first placing a barrel filled with water outdoors. When the water in the barrel was half frozen, pour out the remaining water and remove the barrel. In this way, a transparent hollow ice lantern chimney was formed. Put a candle on the ground and cover it with the ice chimney to protect it from the wind and snow. So, an ice lantern was ready for fishing at night.

The ice lanterns now are vastly different from the primitive ones, in both manufacturing skill and usage. The people in Jilin City have long developed the ice lantern into an art that integrates with sculpture, modeling and architecture. Later, this art spread to Harbin and then to Beijing. Since the 1990s, each year the city would use a dozen thousands of cubic meters of snow and ice to construct an ice-snow street and hold a large-scale ice-lantern gathering. Placed on both sides of the street are ice lanterns of various types, from historic figures to animals and flowers, from classic Chinese pavilions and multistoried structures to world-famous architectures. The ice and snow sculptures are all artworks with features of their own. The candles in the lanterns have been replaced by multicolored and variously shaped electronic lights. Walking among the ice lanterns is like walking through a crystal-line wonderland.

The tradition of lighting and placing lanterns onto the river began in the early Qing Dynasty in Jilin City. Also called "sugar lanterns," the earliest river lanterns were made of braised buckwheat and bran, and the lamp-wicks were with straw dipped into chaff-oil and rice liquor. When lit, the lanterns shone luminously green and sent out thick smoke, adding a sense of mystery to the river at night. Later, people used red paper to make lotus-shaped

lanterns, the bottoms of which were waxed to prevent soaking. The lamp-wicks were also replaced by candles. In the old days, people lit and placed lanterns on the river chiefly on the 15th day of the seventh lunar month. As recorded in the *Annals of Jilin*, "Transport the lotus lanterns on two boats, and then light and release them along with the current. The lanterns appear like thousands of golden lotuses floating on the river. Monks on the boats chant Buddhist sutras, and musicians beat cymbals and drums. Both officials and commoners crowd to watch." From the description, we can deduce that the river-lantern gathering in ancient times was truly a grand and great event.

This tradition has been passed on in Jilin. However, the date is no longer the 15th day of the seventh lunar month, but important festivals and ceremonies, especially the Lantern Festival (the 15th day of the first lunar month). In particular, placing lanterns on the river during the Rime Festival in winter has added new significance and charm to an old tradition. As the Songhua River by Jilin City does not freeze in winter, it is possible to light color lanterns, ice lanterns and river lanterns at the same time. The wonderful and magical scene, with colorful boats and fireworks, provides a joyous atmosphere for the festival. Seen from afar are lines of red lanterns drifting with the flow of the quiet river. The red lotus lanterns and their reflections in the green river shimmer together, along with stars and exploding fireworks flickering over the sky. The sky and the earth are in a state of perfect harmony. The glittering Songhua River becomes another Milky Way. At such times, Jilin becomes a city without night.

Jilin's three types of lanterns, just like the ever-flowing Songhua River, have witnessed the great changes that have taken place in the city, and at the same time have become a symbol of the city's profound culture.

▼ Chemical city in Jilin.

◄ Inside a Catholic church in Jilin City.

▲ Fengman Hydropower Station.

▲ Confucian Temple on Beishan Mountain, Jilin City.

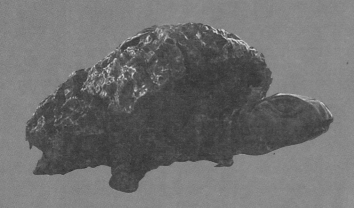

Langmu, A Wood Harder Than Iron and Stone

About 3,000 years ago, after King Wu of the Zhou Dynasty had defeated King Zhou of the Shang court and captured his throne, he ordered the ethnic minority tribes around his country to pay tribute with their special local products. At that time, the Sushen people, living along the middle and lower reaches of the Songhua and the lower reaches of Wusuli and Heilong rivers, had already established relations with the royal court in the Chinese central plains and payed tributes to it. The particular tribute they brought to the royal court are called *hushi shinu*. So, what could the *hushi shinu* in historical records actuality be? King Wu of the Zhou Dynasty had gathered his ministers to identify and locate the tribute from the Sushens. It had a hard shaft and sharp head, but the material was peculiar, neither common metal nor stone. The king asked the Sushen envoy what it was made of, and received the surprising answer: "Wood!" How could wood be so hard! From then on, King Wu always recalled this strange wood when the Sushens were mentioned. In fact, this wood is nothing other than *langmu* (literally, "wood in waves") found drifting along the Songhua and Heilong rivers.

Jilin City is the homeland of *langmu*. Yan Ruoqu of the Qing Dynasty recorded in his *Textual Research on Ancient Articles*, "I once asked a person from Ningguta (old place name in the northeast) about the customs there. He said there is a river called Huntong River, 1,000 *li* to the east. When branches of elm and pine on the banks wither away, they fall into the river, drifting with the waves. No one can tell how many years passed, before the branches transformed into stone. People then made this into arrows. Those transformed from elm branches are the best for making arrows, while those from pine are next best." Then, how exactly were wooden branches transformed

into stone? The story goes like this: In the distant past, the trees on the Songhua and Heilong riverbanks fell into the river after being blown down by strong winds or pushed down by heavy snows. The river water then pounded and compressed the timber hundreds and thousands of times. Particularly on wintry days, when the rivers froze over, the wood would be heavily compressed by the thick ice. Under such circumstances, the timber grew harder and harder. During the spring thaw, massive ice floes moved violently through the rivers. Stuck by the ice, most of timber was bumped onto the banks. Then in summer, the timber would be pounded by the burning sun, after being dried by strong winds. When it turned to winter, they became covered under the snow. Then, when the snow thawed in spring, they would be swept down the rivers again, a new cycle began again. Year after year, this timber finally hardened into "stone."

Th art works of *langmu*, sculpted by nature, possess a variety of forms. Certainly, they have become a unique part of the ice and snow culture, as this special artwork of Jilin is the crystallization of the snow's pressure and river water's pounding. It is also a partner of the cold winds, comrade of the ice and snow, as well as being a child of the freezing river.

▶ *Langmu* root sculpture.

193

Changchun, a Famous Young City

Changchun is the capital of Jilin Province. It also goes by the attractive name of "Spring City," which actually is what it is for northern China. It is like a crystal encased in the rich Songliao Plains.

Changchun is a young city, with a total history of only 200 years. However, dating back 40,000 to 70,000 years ago, there were human beings living along the Songhua and its tributaries, including the Yinma and Yitong rivers. In 1653, the Qing court issued the Statute of Reclamation for Recruiting Farmers in Liaodong. Large numbers of refugees in central China fled to this land. This wave of migration in Chinese history has long been referred to as *Chuang Guandong* (braving a risky journey to the northeast outside the Shanghaiguan Pass for a livelihood). Thereafter, the population steadily increased.

In 1800, the Qing court set up an administrative organ, called the Changchun Prefecture. It is said that, at that time, Chinese roses were blossoming everywhere across the land. The flower, also called the "Changchun flower," gave rise to the name of the prefecture. A different account holds that "Changchun" (Eternal Spring) was so called because its people wished spring would forever remain in this cold northern land.

Changchun is a rising industrial city. It is the cradle of China's automotive industry, photoelectronic technology, biotechnology and applied chemistry. Changchun has produced a multitude of China's firsts: the first *Hongqi* (Red Flag) car, truck, rail coach, rail

wagon, underground electric coach, optical glass, ruby laser generator, electron microscope, laser device, synthetic rubber, etc. So, Changchun has been given many nicknames, including: "automobile city," "science and culture city," "forest city" and "film city."

▲ Cultural Square of Changchun.

▶ A Sculpture in the Sculpture Park of Changchun.

The "Detroit" of China

Changchun is the cradle of China's auto industry. China's first automobile factory was founded on a wasteland in southwest Changchun. After the foundation laying ceremony on 15 July 1953, tens of thousands of construction workers gathered across this area covering dozens of square kilometers. Among them were officials from all around China known for their excellent work, experts returning from abroad, students newly graduated from college, skilled workers from all over the country, and soldiers demobilized from the armed forces just returned from the War to Resist US Aggression and Aid Korea, as well as local farmers. In only three years, these construction workers had built up China's first auto industrial base.

Changchun, although a young city, thus started China's auto industry history, recording a national epic. The first *Jiefang* (Liberation) truck coming of the production line put an end to the history that China could not produce trucks; and the successful development of China's first *Dongfeng* (East Wind) car fulfilled the aspirations of state leaders of the older generation to "take domestically made cars." Thanks to the efforts made by several generations of workers, the First Automobile Works (FAW) has developed into China's largest, most comprehensive and most advanced auto production, research and training center, and become an enterprise group, integrating production, scientific and technological research, marketing, international economic exchange, and foreign trade.

▲ A picture of all brands of vehicles produced by the FAW.
► Changchun International Automobile Fair.

Due to the impressive development of the FAW, Changchun has become China's famed "auto city," lauded as "the 'Detroit' of China." Changchun has developed along with the FAW, from the day the factory was founded on this land. In this city, with a population of 3.12 million, one sixth of its citizens take jobs related to the auto industry, while the FAW itself takes up one seventh of the total area of the city. Someone once said we can witness the progress of China's auto industry in the history of Changchun, covering several generations. Generation after generation of Changchun locals, busy on the auto production lines, laid the foundation for China's auto industry with their blood and sweat. The city is thus very closely tied with vehicles.

▶ FAW's production line for Jetta sedans.
◀ FAW's Century Star sedans of the Red Flag series.
▶ FAW's Bora sedan.

The auto industry in Changchun enjoys a solid foundation in the people. Many Changchun locals know and love cars from childhood. Little children are quite familiar with the names of various cars. August 14, 2005 was the last day of the 10-day 4th China Changchun International Automobile Fair, with a total of over a million people visiting it. On the opening day, elders in wheelchairs from local senior's homes, visited the fair. Perhaps these elders can no longer drive, but their continuing keen interest in cars is rather moving. Now, the fair has become the largest international automobile fair in Northeast Asia. Changchun is now the home of one of China's famed three international automobile fairs (the other two being the Shanghai Automobile Fair and the Beijing Automobile Fair).

"Hollywood" of the East

On a one-million-sq.m plot adjoining the national forest park in southeast Changchun, there is a complex of magical buildings, "Changchun Film Studio Century City," also known as the "'Hollywood' of the East." As China's first world-class theme park combining film-related recreational activities and tourism, the Changchun Film Studio Century City explores a new path for China's film tourism by using all types of advanced film production technology to display Chinese culture. The first phase of the park is made up of ten tourist zones, including high-speed films, children's films, IMAX films, "Dreamland" and laser films, in the hope of briefing the audience with advanced film production technology.

The Changchun Film Studio Century City has become a wonderland and "magic factory," absorbing the essence of the architecture of Universal Studios, Hollywood and Disneyland, integrating a kaleidoscopic range special movie effects. With innovative technologies, thrills, performance and travel experiences, tourists enjoy many world-firsts, including the first water-screen films, and China's first spherical-screen cinema, using the most advanced film technologies of China and even that of the world.

As a center for recreational activities related to film, the Changchun Film Studio Century City does not limit its programs to films. It also provides other special programs developed with cinematic technology, such as representing volcanic eruption from the ancient Mayan civilization and the mystery of the gold coffin of Alexander the Great. The interactive programs allow tourists to experience the magic for themselves. Through high-tech

◀Mao Zedong inspecting the Changchun Film Studio.

methods and special effects in light, sound and electronic, the amusement park makes for a fun-filled world that traditional measures could not provide.

The Changchun Film Studio Century City is a place of great significance, providing the audience with full enjoyment of films and national culture, through the medium of film. It provides visitors with detailed information on the process of making movies. It is totally different from those film studios that offer only fake fronts and backdrops of ancient architectures. Developed by taking full account of the weather of northeast China, all the programs remain open to tourists all year round. It takes tourists about one and a half, to two days, to take in all the programs in the theme park, or at least eight hours if they only wish to enjoy a few of the major ones.

In addition to being a theme park, the Changchun Film Studio Century City will soon become the new site for the Changchun Film Studio, which has, up to now, been located on the banks of Nanhu Lake. Hidden on a piece of beautifully wooded land by the lake, the Changchun Film Studio was China's first film production base. Being the cradle of China's film industry, it is also the first film studio open to tourists. Since its founding, the Changchun Film Studio has produced China's first puppet movie titled *Dream of Being An Emperor*; first popular science film, *Pestilence Prevention*; first animation, *Going After An Easy Prey*; first short feature film, *Bridge*; and first dubbed film, *An Ordinary Soldier*. Since its inception, the studio has produced over 300 art films, several hundred documentary and popular science films, and several hundred dubbed films. More than 100 of the films it produced have been exported to over 40 countries and regions. Furthermore, the Changchun Film Studio has brought forth a large number of movie stars and cinematic artists. The subjects of the films it has produced mirror every aspect of social life, and their artistic style is simple and down to the earth, breathing with life. The studio has a film hall introducing travel tours, and the reproduced scenes include streets of old Beijing and the Yangxin (Cultivating the Mind) Hall in Forbidden City of Beijing, in addition to a hall exhibiting film props and a stunt-show hall. Tourists can also watch the actual shooting of films.

On the east of Kuanping Bridge in Changchun is a "film city," covering about 29 hectares of land. The construction began in 1987 and completed just before the Second China Changchun Film Festival in 1994. The largest of its kind, the "film city" combines film art tours with other recreational activities. When construction of the Changchun Film Studio Century City is completed, both Changchun Film Studio and the Changchun Film City will move into it.

The Changchun Film Festival, held every two years, is a major event jointly sponsored by the people's governments of Jilin Province and Changchun city. Its mission is strengthen friendship and exchange. During the festival, large-scale film-related cultural activities and film shows are held and many movie stars come to the event from all over the world. Besides, large-scale trade fairs and high-tech products exhibitions are held.

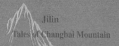

"Imperial Palace" of the Manchukuo Puppet Regime

The "Imperial Palace" of the "Manchukuo" puppet regime is located in the northeast corner of Changchun. It was once the office building of the Bureau of Salt Affairs of Jilin and Heilongjiang. The building and its courtyard may not be as awe-inspiring as an imperial palace, but during its time it was one of the most luxurious buildings in Changchun. Carefully decorated and expanded, the compound was divided into an inner courtyard and outer courtyard. The inner courtyard is the place where puppet emperor Puyi and his family lived. It includes Jixi Tower in the west section, and Tongde Hall, built after 1932, in the east. The outer courtyard was chiefly made up of the Qinmin Hall and Huaiyuan Hall. The palace also had an imperial garden, horserace course, a tennis court, a swimming pool, an air-raid shelter, a railway station for the emperor's special train, and the barracks for the imperial guards, covering 120,000 sq. m in total.

Jixi Tower is where Puyi, his empress Wanrong and his concubine Tan Yulin lived. There are two explanations for how the name came about. One is that it is named after a line in *The Book of Songs*, and means "Brightness." The other is that Puyi named it out of his sincere admiration of his ancestor Emperor Kangxi, wanting to make the Qing Dynasty thrive once again, as his ancestor had done. Inside the building can be found Puyi's bedroom, study and opium room, and Tan Yulin's study and bedroom, as well as a small hall for exhibiting inner court life. In Puyi's bedroom can be seen, sitting on a sofa, waxworks of himself and the so-called "Attaché to the Imperial Household," Yoshioka Yasunori, who was actually a Japanese spy and a colonel of the Kwantung Army directly controlling all of Puyi's activities. In the opium room is a waxwork of the empress Wanrong taking opium on a sofa. A waxwork of Tan Yulin weaving a woolen sweater is found in her study. The mini exhibition of inner court life focuses on the life of Puyi and his wives.

Qinmin Hall was named in line with the doctrine passed down by first Qing emperors. It is the place where the puppet emperor Puyi handled government affairs and gave audience to major ministers and foreign envoys. It is also the place where, on March 1, 1934 Puyi mounted the throne and accepted greetings from his ministers, as well as the very place where the puppet emperor signed the "Japan-Manchukuo Protocol," selling out China's sovereignty over the northeast, met with the young brother of the Japanese emperor, and held talks with Wang Jingwei, a traitor of the Chinese nation who collaborated with Japan. In the "imperial study," where Puyi dealt with government affairs and studied, is a large desk, the emperor's chair (known as "dragon chair" in Chinese) and sofas. In the Taoyan Hall, which served as the banquet hall, there are two long tables placed parallel and high-backed chairs for members of the "imperial family," and a large mirror, in the front of which is the seat with the imperial insignia.

Puyi, known as the last emperor of China, was enthroned and dethroned twice in his life. Once made the puppet emperor of "Manchukuo" by the Japanese aggressors, he was finally remolded into a common Chinese citizen by the People's Republic of China. Born on the 14th day of the first lunar month in 1906, he was the eldest son of Zaifeng, Prince Chun of the Qing Dynasty. At the age of four, he was chosen as crown prince by Empress Dowager Cixi. Soon after, Emperor Guangxu and Empress Dowager Cixi died, and Puyi ascended the throne as Emperor Xuantong of the Qing Dynasty with support from the prince regent. Puyi was forced to abdicate in the Revolution of 1911. Then, in 1917, the warlord general Zhang Xun restored him to the throne for just 12 days. Again, in 1924, he was forced to leave the Forbidden City by the nationalist army general Feng Yuxiang. The following year, he moved to the Japanese Concession in Tianjin, and settled down in Zhangyuan (Garden of the Zhang Family) and then Jingyuan (Garden of Quietness). After the September 18th Incident, Japan occupied the three provinces of northeast China. At the same time, the Japanese tightened up their control over Puyi and sent a collaborationist delegation to "supplicate" him to establish the so-called "Manchukuo" and serve as its "governor." Puyi arrived at Changchun on March 6, 1932 and was installed as the ruler of "Manchukuo" under the reign title "Datong." Changchun, chosen to be the "capital," thus acquired the new name "Xinjing" (new capital). One month later, he moved to the office building of the Bureau of Salt Affairs of Jilin and Heilongjiang, which was then turned into his contemporaneous palace. On March 1, 1934, he was made "emperor" of the "Manchu Empire" under the reign title "Kangde." This was the third time Puyi took the throne, and from then on he became a puppet emperor for 14 years. On August 8, 1945, the Soviet Union declared war on Japan. On the evening of the 14th, Puyi, Wanrong and his other cohorts fled to the Dalizi Iron Mine in Tonghua. When Japan's Emperor Hirohito announced the unconditional surrender on August 15th, Puyi announced his own abdication. He wanted to flee to Japan on August 19th, but was captured at Shenyang Airport, and spent the next five years in prison in the Soviet Union. When Puyi returned to China in 1950, he was sent to the Fushun War Criminal Rehabilitation Camp to be remolded, and was specially pardoned on December 4, 1959. He died of kidney cancer on October 17, 1967.

Time brings great changes to the world. The beginning and end of a period of history always somehow remain shrouded in mystery. The Manchus, who originated in Changbai Mountain, used the mountain as the basis to establish the Qing Dynasty. Coincidently, Puyi, the last emperor of the Qing Empire, descended the throne in Dalizi County at the foot of Changbai Mountain. What a coincidence of history!

City in the Forest

People live in the city, a city that is in a forest. The city itself also contains many woods with beautiful scenery, greenery being found everywhere in the city. This is the eco-environment of Changchun. Changchun has 40 percent of its urban area covered by forest, ranking first in China. In addition to the forests in the urban areas, the 90-km-long and 550-m-wide green belt surrounds the city like a green corridor. Viewed from a plane, this city hidden in the green is inlaid on the Songliao Plains like an emerald. Therefore, Changchun is also called the "Forest City."

People in Changchun are proud of their Jingyuetan National Forest Park nine km from the downtown area, functioning as the "green lungs" of the city. The 4.3-sq. m clear pool glitters like a sapphire in the embrace of the forest. The artificial forest is over 100 sq. km. The hills there are elegant and the water is clear because of the forest; and the city looks beautiful because of the forest. The hills in the park are neither high nor unusual, but they possess natural and undulating outlines much

like a beautiful work of art. Jingyuetan pool is not large, but it has very clear water. The trees in the park were planted by generations of Changchun natives, now ranking as the largest artificial forest in Asia.

In May, the park is ablaze with colorful blossoms of apricot, peach and pear flowers. It is time for various kinds of activities, such as boating, angling, climbing a high tower for a distant view, strolling around the lake and walking through the country fields, all appealing. By mid-summer, green covers the park in different shades. Walking in the forest by the lake, you will feel the humidity of the green cover, even the breeze blowing on the face carries some moisture. It seems the greenness enters your body and lowers the heat of summer. No matter how hot it is outside the forest, inside it remains cool. Jingyuetan Pool in autumn becomes even more charming. It changes all the time. The deep green fades gradually, giving way to yellow, red, purple and brown. Eventually, the color of the hills also turns from light red to vivid red, and finally to deep red. The high and remote blue sky, the floating white clouds, and the gentle breezes place people in a watercolor painting. The pool becomes frozen in winter. At this time, it becomes a fun-filled landscape for outdoor winter activities, including tobogganing, dog-drawn sleds, snowmobiles, horseracing, and ice lanterns. People from all over the world, young and old, male and female, gather here, frolicking in the snow and ice. The China Changchun Jingyuetan Lake Snow and Ice Tourism Festival is held in the park every December. The Sixth Asian Winter Olympics will also be held here in 2007.

Jingyuetan Lake National Forest Park.

▶ A horse-drawn sledge.

▲ Changchun's Jingyuetan Ski Resort.

◀ Snow sculpture.

Huanglongfu City

Huanglongfu (literally "Yellow Dragon City") is sited upon the ancient city of Nong'an. According to historical records, ancient Nong'an was first built at the time of the ancient Fuyu State. In the Han Dynasty, it was the capital of the State of Fuyu. In the Sui Dynasty, it was Fuyu City of Koguryo, and at the time of the Tang Dynasty, it was Fuyu Prefecture of Bohai State. When the Liao Empire destroyed Bohai State, it was renamed "Huanglongfu" and a Huanglong (Yellow Dragon) County was established simultaneously. The name also recalls a legend. In 926, the first year of the Tianxian reign period of the Liao Dynasty, Yelü Abaoji, Emperor Taizu, led his army to attack Bohai State. He first conquered Fuyu City, and then Huhan City, the capital of the Bohai State (Dongjingcheng in Ning'an County, Heilongjiang Province), in the first lunar month of the year, forcing the king of Bohai State to surrender. In the second lunar month, he changed the name of Bohai to "Dongdan" and that of Huhan City to "Tianfu." Later, the emperor returned to Fuyu City with his army, and stayed there because he was ill. In the seventh lunar month, he lay dying. One night, a huge star fell in front of his bedroom hall. At daybreak the following day, a gleaming yellow dragon was seen circling the sky above the city. Then, the dragon flew into the emperor's palace, which was suddenly covered with a purple light and smoke that did not dissipate until evening. Before long, the emperor died, at the age of 55. From then

on, the Liao court renamed Fuyu City "Huanglongfu." This legend was, of course, a conjure-up to exalt Emperor Taizu of Liao Dynasty. Nevertheless, the name "Huanglongfu" was indeed derived from the legend.

In those years, Huanglongfu was one of the seven important strategic towns of the Liao Empire, which were collectively known as "five capitals and two prefectures." Occupying majestically the highland on the west banks of the Yitong River, the city is square in shape, with its city walls running to 3,840 m. Besides the four main gates on the four walls, there is a small gate each on the south, west and east walls. Four high towers stood at the four corners of the city. The famous ancient Nong'an pagoda was built in that period. This octagonal brick pagoda has 13 floors, 33 m high. The earliest Buddhist pagoda in northeast China, it has stood there for more than a thousand years.

As for the building of the pagoda, there are many legends, and one of them goes thus: One night, as the imperial astrologer of the Liao Empire was observing the stars, he saw a meteor falling in the Huanglongfu area. He reported to the emperor that an evil dragon had come down to the world from Heaven to compete with the empire for the control of the country. He suggested that a pagoda should immediately be built to suppress it. On the emperor's orders, he set out immediately for Huanglongfu with a troop of soldiers. After seven days and seven nights' hard journey across the vast grassland, they arrived and lodged at the Longxiang Guesthouse. That very night, the astrologer observed some purple clouds at the east gate of the city going towards the northeast. The next day, accompanied by local officers, he went to the east gate to take a closer look. Out the east gate was a wide river, so he sailed downstream by boat to the north. On the west banks of the river, a continuous mountain range coiled like a dragon for several dozens of miles north of the city. The astrologer believed this was an earth dragon that would enable someone to take the throne. The dragon's head was at the north gate of Xiangzhou City. He believed that, to suppress a dragon, the first step was to suppress its head; therefore he ordered a brick pagoda built outside the north gate of Xiangzhou. However, when this pagoda was only half finished, the astrologer, during nighttime observation, discovered that the earth dragon had turned its head towards the Huanglongfu City. So, he immediately stopped the construction of the pagoda outside Xiangzhou, and led the troops and workers to Huanglongfu to build another pagoda. At that time, the only method to build a pagoda was to pile up a mound. The mound had to be as high as the future pagoda. Three years plus three months plus three days had elapsed in an instant.

Workers heaped up a 39-m-high mound, and finally built a 13-storey brick pagoda outside the west gate of Huanglongfu. Crowned with gold, the pagoda had bronze bells and iron horses hanging down at an angle. Whenever there is wind, the bells and horses jingled in a duet. Later, local people called this pagoda "Longwan (Dragon Bay) Pagoda," and named the pagoda left uncompleted at Xiangzhou "Banjie (Half) Pagoda." Knowing that the earthen dragon had been pacified underneath the pagoda, Emperor Shengzong heaved a sigh of relief. Thereafter, Huanglongfu had got another name, "Long'anfu" (Dragon Peace City).

Maybe the earthen dragon had been suppressed, but the astrologer's forecast did not come true. In a short span of time, the Liao Empire was beaten by the Nüzhen people originating from the Songhua River. When the Nüzhen army conquered Huanglongfu and established the Jin Empire, they set up their capital at Huanglongfu. Then, the Jin Empire set out attacking the Song Dynasty to the south. They finally conquered Kaifeng, capital of the Song Dynasty, in 1126 and captured two emperors of the Song — Emperor Huizong and Emperor Qinzong. When Yue Fei, a hero fighting against the invading force of the Jin Empire in the early stage of the Southern Song, had inspired his generals with the line, "We can drink to our hearts' content when we press forward to Huanglongfu," he was in fact referring to the city we describe here. The remarks of Yue Fei has ever since evolved into a proverb in the Chinese language and passed down.

It is said that, when Wanyan Aguda led his troops to attack Huanglongfu, he was stopped by the Songhua River, over which there were no boats at all then and there. With no other way around, he pointed with his whip to the opposite side and ordered his troops to ford the river in the direction he pointed. He was surprised that the river water only reached the horses' abdomens. After the army had successfully crossed the river, he sent somebody to survey the river again. It was discovered that the river was unbelievably fathomless. To commemorate this successful crossing, in 1140 the Jin royal court ordered the name of Huanglongfu be changed to "Jizhou," and then to "Long'an," and soon back to "Huanglongfu." In the late Ming Dynasty, this region became a grassland for the Mongolians. In 1889, the Qing court officially set up the Nong'an County, a name that has been passed down to this day. Nong'an is a homonymic of "Long'an," meaning "Dragon Peace." In folklore, it is also called "Longwan," and was also known as Nong'an Fort.

Both the Liao Empire and Jin Empire have become something in the past. After so many years, only the ancient pagoda stands. Many stories about the pagoda have spread among the locals. As to why the pagoda leans, the locals may tell you an interesting story. When Emperor Shengzong of the Liao ordered to have the pagoda built, he stored a large quantity of gold under it. An veteran Taoist from the south discovered the secret at a glance, and he declared that he could pull down the pagoda with 50 pointed-horn bulls to capture the gold foal hidden in it. A greedy landlord was eager for the wealth, and he looked everywhere for bulls with pointed horns. However, every time he managed to amass 50 such bulls, one of them would die. It turned out that the local people poisoned the bull in the hope to protect the gold foal. Under this situation, this greedy landlord grew too impatient to wait any longer. He had the 49 bulls he had pull at the pagoda. However, the pagoda did not fall although it was tilted. The anxious man yoked the bulls together to himself to pull the pagoda, but he still failed. Just then, a round gold mirror fell from the top of the pagoda and rolled away. The landlord immediately chased after it. He was so caught up in chasing after the rolling gold mirror that he did not watch his way. When the mirror rolled into the river, he too fell into it and was washed away. Nevertheless, the pagoda became tilted to this day.

Huge Crowds Watching "Two-person Song and Dance Duet"

In Jilin Province, as in everywhere in the entire northeast China, many people are fans of *er'renzhuan* (Two-person Song and Dance Duet), a traditional form of folk opera very much popular there.

Er'renzhuan has its origin among the common people of northeast China. It is the epitome of a distinctive local art form. As early as several hundred years ago, with its flexible and vivid style, *er'renzhuan* was performed inside the huts of hunters, ginseng diggers and gold-miners, as well as in the yards of farmers. This popular opera has long been the favorite of the Jilin people, who always say, "We'd rather give up a meal than

▲ Stage photo of Snow in the Northeast (Jilin Opera).

▶ *Er'renzhuan* performers of the northeast.

miss a *er'renzhuan* performance."

In *er'renzhuan*, one actor and one actress would usually act out a number of characters, singing and dancing, on and off the stage. The performance is vibrant and eventful, filled with great local country flavor. Though called *er'renzhuan* (which literally means "two-person rotation"), very often more than two players are needed in a performance.

Generally speaking, the performance of *er'renzhuan* is divided into three styles: *danchutou* (one-person performance), *er'renzhuan* (two-person duet) and *lachangxi* (short folk plays calling for more than two performers). In *danchutou*, there is only one player who acts the different characters in a changing and animated way, while in *lachangxi* it involves more than two people but with a young female actress and male clown playing the leading role, and retains the lively unique flavor and performing style of *er'renzhuan*.

Over hundreds of years, *er'renzhuan* has acquired its own distinctive skills, commonly known as "four skills and one secret," namely, singing, speaking, acting, and dancing, as well as a unique skill. *Er'renzhuan* opera uses informal and candid language, as well as melodic local accents, to impact people's daily lives and make the audience's emotions flow with the players' actions, words and performances. All the tunes and tones employed in the singing come across as warm, intimate and heartfelt. Originating from and spreading among the common folks, the repertoire of *er'renzhuan* includes such time-honored operettas as *Fifth Watch of A Crescent Night*, *White Jasmine* and *Young Scholar Strolls in A Temple*. The dialogue in *er'renzhuan*, also called "shuokou" (speaking), is also divided into different types, such as "taozikou" (set dialogues), "gedakou" (blurts) and "zhuankou" (witty dialogue). The local people thoroughly enjoy the vivid and lively language, the smart and humorous dialogues and down-to-earth plots. The acting in *er'renzhuan* is also referred to as "doing," to fully energize the performances to attract

people's attention and emotional response, a unique feature of the opera. *Er'renzhuan* performance requires that "if two persons act the same character, the character must remain the same though the players are different," "if a player acts various characters, the characters must be different though there is only one player," etc. No matter how complex the plot is, no matter how many characters, no matter how grand the scene, there are usually only two players in one play: one female, and one clown. They act out the old and young, male and female characters, on and off the stage. The changes of character are frequent but appear seamless and natural. The players must attempt to use their range of acting skills so that each character shows to the full his or her own different spirit. The dancing in *er'renzhuan* is very special, especially in skills of the wrists. The diverse wrist movements are truly dazzling. Besides the wrist skills, also very important in *er'renzhuan* performance are the shoulder skills, waist skills and various feet movements. The "unique skill" mentioned above involves the use of a handkerchief or fan. A small handkerchief becomes a living being in the hands of *er'renzhuan* performers, sometimes resembling a rotating wheel or an instruction flag, and at other times flying high or falling slowly. The small fan is also no mere prop, as it can change into different forms, attracting people's attention.

Yangge dance of the northeast. ▼

Foods of Jilin

Some people say, if you want to know a place or a city, the best way is to taste its food. A folk saying goes like this: "Get food from a mountain if you live by a mountain, and get food from a river if you live by a river." The people in Jilin, living by Changbai Mountain and the Songhua River, have created their unique Jilin cuisine.

A Dish Braised in A Big Pot

Everybody knows the unique Jilin dish called "braised pork with starch noodles," a traditional dish in fact loved by all people in northeast China, where the average households often cook this dish for dinner. The ingredients could be very simple, just a kilogram of pork and several bundles of starch noodles. Braised with sauce, the dish is delicious when its aroma wafts over, even before it is ready to be served.

The traditional way to take "braised pork with starch noodles" is to suck the noodles into the mouth, making some noise. This may not sound refined viewed from the perspective of modern civilization, yet it simply shows off an aspect of the uninhibited nature of the Jilin people. Of course, women are usually more reserved than men, who always suck starch noodles in by the mouthful.

Although "braised pork with starch noodles" is basically a popular homemade dish, the ingredients, including the duration of cooking and even the color of the dish, are chosen with care. Streaky pork should be used. With both lean and fat meat, the braised pork would possess a good chewy texture. If only lean meat is used, the braised pork would be tough. And if only fat meat is used, it would be greasy. Put the pork into the pot before the water is heated. In this way, the oil in the pork would braise into the soup and the pork will not taste greasy. Then, cut the pork into slices. The slices should not be too thin, as thin pork slices would easily break up into small pieces. However, it is neither good to cut it too thick. Dried starch noodles made of potato are best for the dish, because potato-starch noodles tolerate a relatively long period of braising, which improves the taste.

"Braised pork with starch noodles" is the most representative of Jilin specialties. Jilin people like braising. They braise almost every kind of food, braising potatoes with eggplant, potatoes with beans, Chinese cabbage with beancurd, and so on. A limerick widespread in the Changbai Mountain area goes thus: "When eating braised catfish with eggplant, even old men eat till bursting at the seams." In braised hotpots, the addition of certain mountain delicacies nicely improves the food's tonic effects. This is a feature of Jilin food unmatched by other local foods.

Another simpler dish is "braised river fish in river water." Jilin is a land of fish and rice, abundant in freshwater fish. Fish found in the Songhua River, such as bream and crucian carp, are exceptionally delicious. The traditional way adopted by the fishermen to cook fish is to braise the river fish in river water. The fish must be alive. Scrape the scales and clean the fish, then put it into a pot full of river water to braise. Never fry it beforehand. The ingredients are only salt, shallots and ginger. As the folk saying goes, "One thousand boils of bean curd and ten thousand boils of fish"; Because when the fish is braised a long time, the soup turns milky white and tastes extremely nice. With a dash of ginger and vinegar, this goes excellently with wine.

Jilin people love braised food, whether at home, in restaurants, or even on the streets. In Baishan City, one can witness a most eye-catching scene of numerous large pots braising pickled vegetables in the open air.

Why braising? Many people believe that braised food is effective in resisting cold and allaying hunger. In the cold weather of the Changbai Mountain region, hot braised food indeed warms up people. Yet, the most conspicuous advantage of braised food is its convenience. One or two braised dishes are enough for a household meal. Jilin people claim not to have enough patience to make more delicate foods; their generally quick tempers finding it troublesome and time wasting. Typical braised dishes, including "stewed white pork and blood sausage," "braised chicken with mushrooms," "braised chops," as well as "beans and corn with wide starch noodles," all demonstrate Jilin people's nature as not wanting to bother about trivia. From this perspective, "braised pork with starch noodles" is not only a dish, but also a lifestyle.

Some also think that the characteristics of Jilin dishes may be summed up in two words, "fiery heat." From the direct contact with fire of the hotpot and roast, and indirect contact with fire to braise dishes, and even Jilin people's love of strong liquor, Jilin people hope to gain some extra heat along with enjoying the delicious food, to resist the local cold climate. With hot tempers, Jilin people create hot Jilin dishes and also lead fiery lives.

Fiery Hotpot

In the north, when the white snow cover the land, it is very comforting for a family to crowd around a hotpot and enjoy a marvelous dinner. Hotpot is a cooking implement made of metal or pottery. It is round, with a small chimney in the center into which people put charcoal to keep the soup around the chimney boiling. People place sliced meat and vegetables in the soup to cook. When the food is cooked, they fish it out to eat while hot.

There are many conventions for enjoying hotpot, such as "flying in front and walking in the back," "fish to the left and shrimp to the right," and "scatter vegetables around." "Flying" refers to fowls like chicken or duck, while "walking" means meat such as of deer, boar, cow and sheep. "Fish to the left and shrimp to the right" is an unchangeable rule. In Jilin, the hotpot is not only a big serving dish when guests come, it is also used as a daily soup dish. Soup is considered necessary in the diet, along with fried or braised food. The hotpot makes the best soup. Northeasterners love to eat pickled Chinese cabbage, which is refreshing with its dash of sour. Place shredded pickled Chinese cabbage into bone soup in a red copper hotpot, and then instantly boil to boil pre-cooked meat. This is a popular hotpot in Jilin. With the pickled vegetable, the meat turns very tender but not feeling greasy. Blood sausage, unique to northeast China, is also a marvelous ingredient for hotpot, especially when boiled together with pickled vegetable and fatty meat. Of course, the hotpots served to guests contain more delicacies. If the guests are welcomed visitors, the host will serve the hotpot in accordance with the rules of "flying in front and walking at the back" and "fish to the left and shrimp to the right," and the guests will discern the host's warmth on seeing this. If the host does not appreciate the visitors, other hotpot serving methods are used to politely make them aware of this, e.g., placing two large meatballs in the front and game meat in the back, would imply "please leave!" Tactful visitors would immediately depart.

In fact, the Jilin custom of using the hotpot to either warmly or coldly treat their guests is a dietary representation of a tradition that has integrated the cultures of central and northeast China. Chinese people always express their emotions in more reserved ways, being a basic general characteristic. This is also embodied in other aspects of life, for example in *chawan zhen* (tea-cup arrangement) or *yancha zhen* (tobacco and tea arrangement) customary to trade associations of the past. Similar to hotpot, both refer to the manner of setting out the pipes and teacups when serving visitors. Given the extraordinarily cold weather in the northeast, alcohol and tea are always served in interactions between people, including among traditional trade associations. The hosts and guests both indicate what they want to say through the placement or moving of vessels for alcohol and tea or tobacco. This is called *yinxue* (inference), used with similar connotations in language. When someone malicious was to visit, the chief would tell his men, "He is coming, repulse him." The repulse goes like this: the host serves two bowls of tea, one half-full and the other deliberately overflowing. The visitor will leave as soon as he sees this. If the host serves a bowl of water and a bowl of tea at the same time, this signifies a welcome, and the visitor must splash the water on the floor, and then drink the tea slowly. If the visitor makes a mistake, the host puts his pipe across the two bowls, meaning "the friendship is over," and his men will drive the visitor away.

The hotpot reflects the hospitality and loyalty of northeasterners to friends and comrades. They share food together, as well as sharing happiness and suffering together. Of course, in the present day, every family can cook hotpot no matter what the season; and the rules are also no longer so strict.

Restorative Mountain Delicacies

In addition to streaky pork, long potato-starch noodles, braised food and hotpot, people in Jilin Province also love wild herbs, hedgehog fungus and wild ginseng from Changbai Mountain.

Wild herbs found on Changhai Mountain are much liked by the Jilin People. Although

Mountain delicacies of Jilin.

people in Jilin today have no lack of fish and meat, they still like eating certain wild herbs sometimes. It is unnecessary to merely utter the famed "three treasures of northeast," for many of the wild herbs that the locals eat are strange to most other people. These wild herbs, dug up from the areas around the nature reserves, are a type of unique yet delicious organic food, free from pollutants, with China Sanicle, Manyprickle Acathopanax root and bracken being the most commonly seen. Such edible wild plants thrive in the lower areas of the mountains, and are easy to collect as well as most flavorful. In spring, people coming to Jilin will have the chance to enjoy the freshest wild herbs; while in summer there are only dehydrated or dried ones. Jilin boasts a large variety of edible funguses, such as black fungus, golden oyster mushroom, hedgehog fungus, chicken mushroom, broom mushroom and pig-mouth mushroom. As for unique products of Changbai Mountain, like ginseng, pine mushroom, deer tendon and wood-frog placenta, they are both rare medicines as well as delicacies on dining table.

Wild herbs are important ingredients for Jilin-style dishes. Almost 80 percent of all the ingredients for Jilin dishes, including all the staple foods and condiments, are from Changbai Mountain. As having mountain delicacies is in accord with the modern dietary ideas of "natural, green, nutritious, healthy," Jilin-style dishes that largely use such ingredients have turned out to be the No.1 among the eight new-style cuisines recently appeared in China.

One Jilin-style dish, called "quick-boiled hazel grouse with pine mushrooms," has a tasty and mellow soup. Pine mushroom is a unique product of Changbai Mountain. The best season to have pine mushroom is autumn. No matter fresh or pickled, the mushroom's taste is excellent with its soft and tender flesh. As early as the Ming Dynasty, people discovered its nutritious value. At that

time, 50 grams of dried pine mushroom could exchange for about two kilograms of rice.

Almost all parts of the sika deer in Changbai Mountain are considered treasures. Its tendons can strengthen people's muscles and bones, and are hence good for health. "Oiled deer tendons with onion" is one such dish. Together with "chicken-leg onion" produced in the region around Changbai Mountain, cooked deer tendons taste particularly nice. Another dish, "assorted deer treasures casserole," contain the deer's tendons, tail, tongue, lips, ears, blood, spine, heart and antlers. Braised into a specially thick soup, the casserole is both tasty and nutritious.

"Braised black-boned chicken with ginseng" is a traditional medicinal dish. It is a nutritious dish particularly suited for autumn and winter. If you persevere in eating it regularly, it will help you stay healthy and to live long. Ginseng is a unique product of Changbai Mountain. In the past, it was considered a "divine medical herb," said to be able to prolong people's lives, and even revive the dead. The Manchus, who cherished this herb very much, introduced it to the Chinese central plains after they took control of the entire country. Legend has it that, every time before Emperor Kangxi went into a battle, he would have a black-boned chicken braised with ginseng to provide him sufficient energy. In those years, ginseng was only taken as one auxiliary ingredient in the dishes and could not be eaten alone. Now, the Jilin people have developed a number of dishes using ginseng as the major ingredient, which are not only unique but also extremely delicious.

"Braised bear's paw with ginseng" used to be a dish specially reserved for the rich and powerful, because the paws of bears were hard to get. Now, the state has banned hunting of bears, so the restaurants use beef tendons instead.

◄ Green edible wild herbs.

▲ Black fungus.

► Green in wild fields.

【 Concluding Remarks 】

As early as 5,000 years ago, the ancestors of humans left their first traces in Jilin. Over 3,000 years ago, the Sushen people, who carried large bows, joined in ceremonial gatherings of tribal heads in Chinese central plains, and brought with them, as tributes to the royal court, arrows made of hard wood and reindeer. About 360 years ago, the Manchus, descendants of the Sushen people, established China's last feudal empire — the Qing. Over 200 years ago, groups upon groups of extremely creative and resilient people from the central plains took refuge in Jilin. They gathered ginseng, logged timber, rafted on rivers, and lived in the boundless forests and on the vast plains. More and more people living south of Shanhaiguan Pass were drawn to this fertile land. They multiplied there and created a world that belongs to them. The offspring of these migrants and the aboriginal people of Jilin have worked together to create a new history. Today, the Jilin people, who have inherited their ancestors' generosity, courage, sincerity and wisdom, are exploring new ways toward greater happiness.

Human pursuit of happiness never ends. During the first Five-Year Plan (1953-57), Jilin launched its initial development with great achievements. Now 50 years later, the state's strategic decision to rejuvenate the old industrial bases in the northeast has once again pushed Jilin to the forefront. Carrying the hopes of 27 million people, Jilin has entered into its cycle of development. Across the hope-filled vast land of Jilin, unprecedented reforms are being carried out, and a promising rejuvenation is on its way.

Jilin has a bright future, as a land red hot and primed for investment. Jilin is a land of luck, filled with countless opportunities.

Jilin extends its welcome to friends from all corners of the world!

Appendices

Geographical Location and Climate of Jilin Province

Jilin Province, abbreviated as "Ji," is located between 121° 38' E and 131° 19' E, and 40° 52' N and 46° 18' N, in the middle of northeast China. The longest spans west to east stretch across almost 750 km, and north to south about 600 km. It is 187,400 sq. km in area, about 2 percent of China's total.

Jilin is located at the center of northeast Asia, which comprises Japan, part of Russia, the Democratic People's Republic of Korea, the Republic of Korea, Mongolia and northeast China. It borders Russia in the east, as well as the Democratic People's Republic of Korea across the Yalu River and Tumen River in the southeast. The borderline is 1,438.7 km altogether, of which the borderline with Russia is 232.7 km, and that with the DPRK is 1,206 km. It is connected with Liaoning Province in the south, Inner Mongolia in the west, and Heilongjiang in the north.

Huichun City in the east of the province is the geometrical center point of northeast Asia. It is 15 km away from the Nippon Sea and four km from the Posjet Bay in Russia. Changchun, the capital of the province, is where the transport lines of northeast Asia all intersect.

Situated in the mid-latitudes of the Northern Hemisphere, east of Eurasia, and at the same time in the most northern part of China's temperate zone and close to the sub-frigid zone, the climate of eastern Jilin is damp with a lot of rainfall, as it is close to the Yellow Sea and Nippon Sea; whereas its western part is dry, being farther from the sea and closer to the dry Mongolian Plateau. The province has an obvious temperate continental monsoon climate. Rain falls during the hot season, and the four seasons noticeably differ. Spring is dry and windy, summer is hot and rainy, and autumn has clear skies and breezy days, while winter is long and cold. The mean temperature in most of the province is 35.6- 42.8°F (2-6 °C). It boasts 2,200 to 3,000 hours of sunshine every year, which provide 4,892°F (2,700 °C) to 5,792°F (3,200 °C) in annual cumulative temperature, sufficient for the growth of crops of one season. The annual precipitation is between 400 and 900 mm. From east to west, the climate changes from humid to semi-humid to semi-arid. In the west of the province, the frost-free period is about 150 days, and in the eastern mountainous area, about 130 days. Frost starts appearing in late September, and ends in late April to mid-May.

Major Organizations of Foreign Affairs

Overseas Chinese Affairs Office of the People's Government of Jilin Province	86-431-2711154
Information Office of the People's Government of Jilin Province	86-431-8904006
Department of Commerce of Jilin Province	86-431-5676242
Jilin Province Tourism Administration	86-431-8906806
People's Association for Friendship with Foreign Countries of Jilin Province	86-431-2766209
The Center for Overseas Cultural Exchanges of Jilin Province	86-431-8904011
Overseas Exchange Association of Jilin Province	86-431-2768382
Jilin Branch of China Council for Promotion of International Trade	86-431-8549432
Changchun Customs	86-431-4601930

Major Websites

China Jilin	www.chinajilin.com.cn
Jilin Information Center	www.ji.cninfo.net
Changchun Information Center	www.changchun.gov.cn
Jilin Tourist Information Center	www.gojl.com.cn

Major News Agencies

Jilin Daily	www.chinajilin.com.cn[z1]
Jilin Radio	www.jlradio.com.cn
Jilin TV	www.jltv.net
New Culture Paper	www.xwhb.net
City Evening News	www.chinajilin.com.cn/cswb
Economic and Trade News of East Asia	www.chinajilin.com.cn/dyxw

Major Hotels

City	Hotel	Star	Telephone	Address
Changchun	Shangri-la Hotel	5★	86-431-8981818	9 Xi'an Road
	Redbuds Hotel	5★	86-431-5685540	138-1 Renmin St.
	Noble Hotel	5★	86-431-5622888	89 Renmin Street
	Paradise Hotel	4★	86-431-2090999	72 Renmin Street
	International Conference Center	4★	86-431-4618888	102 Ziyou Ave.
	Song Yuan Hotel	4★	86-431-2727001	21 Xinfa Road
	Changbaishan Hotel	4★	86-431-5588888	18 Xinmin Street
	Changchun Hotel	4★	86-431-8791888	10 Xinhua Road
	Maxcourt Hotel	4★	86-431-8962688	19 Xian Road
	Changchun Overseas Chinese Hotel	4★	86-431-5599888	1 Hubin Road
	Jilin Province Hotel	3★	86-431-8488999	72 Renmin Street
	Hawaii Hotel	3★	86-431-5296368	66 Ziyou Ave.
Jilin	Century Swissbel Hotel	5★	86-432-2168888	77 Jilin Street
Yanbian	Baishan Hotel	4★	86-433-2515956	2 Youyi Road
Siping	Jiping Hotel	4★	86-434-3249166	104 Xinhua St.
Tonghua	Tonghua Hotel	4★	86-435-3207666	309 Cuiquan Road
Baicheng	Jihe Hotel	4★	86-436-3677666	North Jihe Plaza Liaoyuan
Liaoyuan	City Hotel	3★	86-437-5088881	6 Longshan Rd. N.
Songyuan	Qian Gorlos Hotel	3★	86-438-2122988	21 Wulan Street
Baishan	Baishan City Hotel	3★	86-439-3594888	102 Hunjiang St.

图书在版编目（CIP）数据

吉林：白山松水情 / 刘乃季 林毅 杨有海主编.

北京: 外文出版社, 2006（全景中国）

ISBN 7-119-04516-4

I. 吉... II. 杨... III. 吉林省 - 概况 - 英文 IV.K923.4

中国版本图书馆 CIP 数据核字（2006）第 078121 号

全景中国 — 吉林：白山松水情

主　　编：刘乃季 林　毅 杨有海

撰　　稿：王　颖 刘春光

图片提供：吉林省人民政府新闻办公室

　　　　　吉林省文化传播策划制作中心

中文审定：王传民

责任编辑：雷喜红

翻　　译：严　晶 王　琴 周晓刚 曲　磊 欧阳伟萍 冯　鑫

英文审定：May Yee 李振国

装帧设计：蔡　荣

内文设计：姚　波

印刷监制：韩少乙

© 2006　外文出版社

出版发行：

外文出版社（中国北京百万庄大街 24 号）

邮政编码 100037　http://www.flp.com.cn

制　　版：

外文出版社照排中心

印　　制：

北京京都六环印刷厂

开本：980mm × 710mm 1/16（平装）印张：15.5

2006 年第 1 版第 1 次印刷

（英）

ISBN 7-119-04516-4

09800

85-E-615P